HEARTS
IN THE
ICE

HEARTS
IN THE
ICE

The Adventures of the First Two Women
to Overwinter Solo in Svalbard

Sunniva Sorby & Hilde Fålun Strøm

CONTENTS

PROLOGUE

We shall not cease from exploration
And the end of all our exploring
Will be to arrive where we started
And know the place for the first time.
— T.S. Eliot, "Little Gidding"

It's mid-November and freezing cold: -22°C (about -8°F). We are in the middle of what's called the "polar night"—when the sun dips more than 6° below the horizon so that the night lasts for more than twenty-four hours. We'll have about three months of this polar night; that means three months of complete darkness. Light—Arctic twilight—will start to reappear in early February when the sun eventually creeps up over the horizon, but we won't see it pop over the mountain range until March 8. None of this stops us from venturing outside. We seem to live to feel the sharp sting of cold and the sudden brush of Arctic wind on our cheeks. It makes us feel completely alive.

When the day is as dark as the night, there's no way to tell if it's morning or evening. We survive by establishing a routine. We get up; we go for walks with Ettra; we eat meals at regular times. We train and sleep at regular times. Without a routine, we would easily get out of sorts. If we stand outside and look to the east and west, the north and south, there are no streetlights, no warm glow from a porch light: we have no neighbors for 140 kms (87 miles). There's absolutely nothing to tell us where we are.

Neither are there any bushes or trees here in the Arctic. Our cabin, Bamsebu, lies at the mouth of the Van Keulenfjorden, a fjord 30 km (19 miles) long, and we're surrounded by mountains in all directions—gorgeous, majestic mountains whose layers of rock pressed skyward over millions of years, revealing geological epochs. The layers run diagonally, giving the mountains beautiful bands in every shade of dark brown and even red, white, grey, or black. A geologist's dream. The northern lights—the mysterious and truly magnificent aurora borealiz—dance above us often. We will never tire of this aurora light, which often showers us with its rays. At 100 km (62 miles) away, the lowest band of aurora are closer than the town of Longyearbyen.

A seasoned, respected journalist friend of ours, Arne O. Holm, observed that our transition to Bamsebu and this old-school way of living must have been more difficult than the pioneers' adjustments back in the fifties. We left a busy, fragmented daily life with our senses overloaded by noise, lights, TV, computers, and constant motion. To live simply, disconnected from all to-dos and noise, seems impossible for many people today, but we transitioned into a life with no running water and no insulation, which required us to chop wood for heat and collect ice and snow for cooking and drinking, all in total isolation. A simple life. A life with purpose and thoughtfulness. This existence at Bamsebu has required recalibration and major adjustments.

Something happens in this apartness from the rest of the world and in the dark. It's as if the deepest parts of your soul start to awaken, your senses are heightened, and a soft calm prevails. You feel at peace. We discovered that anything we couldn't now see with our own eyes, we could remember—colors, shapes, flowers, plants, animals, and all the magic out there. We also discovered that, as the darkness wears on, anything unresolved in your heart will find its way to the surface: insecurities, fears, and doubts come gently crawling out. In stillness and quiet solitude, you discover hidden parts of yourself, whether you like it or not.

Most of us have had that "aha" moment of silence and grounding. Think back to a time you spent outside in nature, when the busyness seemed to melt away and things just seemed so darn simple. You weren't swarmed by pings, buzzes, or vibrations—it was just you and your hiking boots. Only after spending several days this way can you start to feel yourself again, hear your own thoughts, and reclaim control over your wants and needs. Today, more than ever, our minds and beliefs seem to be hijacked by commercials and noise—and so, today, more than ever, seeking out a slice of solitude and quiet has become crucial to our well-being, a matter of survival. To ditch your cell phone every now and again is very freeing—and at Bamsebu, we faced a year of being cell-phone free. Pure bliss.

If you stare at something long enough, you commit it to memory. We know where the side of the hill to our east meets the ridge whose spine stretches south to north. We remember that ridge from the two weeks we spent here in August 2019, orienting ourselves and getting set up here at Bamsebu. It was summer, and we were experiencing the spectacular midnight sun: twenty-four hours of daylight. We were unpacking and sorting through our gear when we saw him: *Ursus maritimus*, a huge white polar bear, lumbering slowly up toward the ridge. He took a few steps, then tilted his head to look our way as if he knew we were here. Over the course of our year living in this Arctic wilderness, we would have more than sixty polar bear encounters, some right outside the hut. The closest was two meters (six and a half feet) from where we stood. We often wonder how many more polar bears snuck past the hut during the dark polar night, leaving only paw prints that were quickly covered by the blowing snow. We will never know.

Ettra is our three-year-old Malamute, weighing in at roughly 40 kgs (90 pounds). We've often been asked if we have her here for safety against the polar bears—as an early warning system of sorts; after all, she can bark. We brought her here first and foremost because she is a great companion and second for safety. She only lets out a bark if she can smell or hear a polar bear. Otherwise, she is a strong, hard sleeper. Her head is about as big as a polar bear's nose.

When it's dark out, the element of surprise is everywhere. We always, always hope for the best and prepare for the worst. We wear heavy cold-weather gear, bulky insulated boots, headlamps that illuminate up to 200 meters (650 feet) away, two pairs of gloves, a rifle over the shoulder, and a thick belt with a revolver, flare gun, and Swiss tool. The Iridium satellite phone stays tucked inside one of our jacket pockets. This is us going for a walk in the polar night. Hope for the best, prepare for the worst. Our walks are short, our steps calculated, and our heads always turning in all directions to see what's out there. One thing you don't want is to meet a polar bear in the dark when it's windy, your visibility is limited by snowfall, a whiteout, and you're on foot.

After several weeks of feeling tethered and a bit limited by the darkness, we decide it's time to take a snowmobile ride over the ridge to the west. It's a freeing thought. Just getting ready for such an outing brings its own excitement.

For the first time, we decide to leave Ettra tied up outside Bamsebu. There's a tiny sliver of light beginning to show, and no wind, but it's still cold at -13°C (9°F). We put our snowmobile suits on over all of our layers, balaclavas under our helmets, neck gaiters, and gloves, and bring extra headlamps, a thermos of hot water, and our belts with flare guns, knives, Swiss tools, and revolvers around our waists.

We pull the cover off our Lynx snowmobile; loosen its skis from their frozen grip; stash our photo equipment, sat phone, and a few extras into the back hatch; tuck our rifle in its holster, which is mounted at the side of the snowmobile; and take one last look at Ettra, then head off to the ridge. It takes us about ten minutes to get to the back of the ridge, where we set up our tripod. Of course, the wind reappears just as we began our little photoshoot, so we only take a few timed shots of us with the Lynx and a hint of light behind us before heading back. In the photo, we're just two black silhouettes, but the hint of color is an exciting indicator that a new time is coming: the awakening of the Arctic.

The snowmobile has its own light, but we also scan left to right with a high-beam flashlight as we ride. Of course, we want to see Ettra as soon as possible. Leaving her behind feels like leaving our firstborn for the first time, though it's only been thirty minutes. We wonder if she's missed us: Did she sit up and wait for us the entire time? Did she find peace and lie down? Did she howl until she couldn't hear the snowmobile? We'll never know.

As we draw closer to the cabin, our lights hit something directly in front of it. It's big and white—and it's not Ettra. It takes a couple of seconds before it sinks in. It couldn't be . . . could it? . . . A POLAR BEAR!? As we come closer still, our suspicions are confirmed. The bear just stands there. Huge. Towering. Majestic. It dwarfs our Bamsebu—even on all fours, from our distance, it seems like it's about the height of our roofline.

But where the f**k is Ettra?

Hilde speeds toward the cabin at full throttle, our hearts pounding out of our chests. Then we see something red on the ground. A horrid thought comes over both of us: *Has something happened to Ettra?* We're still a few hundred meters from the cabin, but we both shout out: "EEEEEETTTTTTRRRRRRRRAAAAA."

We need to see her.

The polar bear stands completely still, just staring at us.

Shouldn't it move? Shouldn't it throw itself around and disappear into the darkness? But there's no reaction.

It stands completely frozen, fixed on us as we come flying over the snow-covered tundra. Our snowmobile roars, and the spotlight shines bright, but the polar bear stays still, standing on all fours.

Hilde eases up on the gas and swerves to the right. We're much closer to the cabin now, but we still can't see Ettra. Fear is pumping through the both of us. "ETTRA!!" we shout again. Coming closer on high speed, we see that the red color we saw in the snow is just the long red case for our UNIS ice-core drill bit; we both breathe a sigh of relief. Do we need to maneuver to prevent a collision? Seriously?? A second later we see Ettra sitting just a few meters from the massive bear. A rather unbelievable sight.

We—and Ettra—were seconds away from something horrid and devastating happening. Ettra backs up against the front door and starts to bark frantically. She's extremely stressed, and it only takes us half a second to kick into survival mode. We have to get the polar bear away from Ettra, urgently. Hilde speeds up the Lynx, but he still doesn't budge. How will we get him out of here? Hilde inches the Lynx even closer, but still nothing. Are you kidding me? He still won't leave.

We'll never know what suddenly spooks him, but eventually he takes off. We set the flare gun off in the direction he was running, hoping it will serve as another warning to stay away. By this point, we're practically frozen.

Ettra jumps all over us. Oh, the story she could tell if she could speak— God knows what she's been through. We want to retrace the polar bear's steps, but first, we wrap ourselves around Ettra and make sure she's okay. We're relieved and still a little in shock—just two months earlier, a desperately hungry polar bear killed a dog in Hornsund, a research station approximately 150 km (95 miles) to the south. Ettra is shaken, and she's peed on the front porch in fear, but she doesn't have a scratch on her. And frankly, who wouldn't pee their pants if they were cornered by a polar bear standing a few feet away? We both feel a little guilty that she was all alone. It could have been fatal.

After hugging Ettra again and again and again, we set out on a mission to find out: *Where had it come from? Which direction? And how big are its footprints?* We were only gone for thirty minutes. Did it stalk us and wait for us to leave? Or did it stumble upon our cabin by coincidence? We follow its tracks as best we can and measure its footprint at 62 cm (two feet). The wind is kicking up the snow, so we have to move fast to follow the tracks before they get covered up. We discover that the bear approached the cabin on the exact route where we had walked with Ettra just an hour before we left. What a close call.

Riding back toward Bamsebu after trying to follow the bear's incoming tracks, we can hear Ettra barking. Luckily, there are no uninvited visitors this time. We undo her chain, put her on a leash, and all three of us walk around Bamsebu to assess our visitor's movements. We determined that it walked up to the front door; tipped over a food barrel that had chocolate and coffee in it; sniffed the top of another one, leaving a snout print; put its big paw on a cooler; and walked all around Bamsebu. Still, we have many unanswered questions. *How long was it here? It must have been right on top of her. Was it her bark that scared it off? Why was it not at all fazed by the snowmobile?*

But there's one thing we knew for certain: The polar bear will be back. All 600 kg (1,300 lbs) of it.

INTRODUCTION

THE ADVENTURE OF A LIFETIME

The real voyage of discovery consists not in seeking
new landscapes, but in having new eyes.
— Marcel Proust

SUNNIVA

In 2010, I began to work on a book I titled *The Will of the Wind*. I wrote nine chapters, had it professionally edited, and then tucked it neatly inside a desk drawer. It has been tucked away ever since. I titled the final chapter, "Antarctica Speaks Out." It was a call to action, urging readers to pay attention to the profound changes we had been witnessing south of 57 degrees of latitude on the Antarctic continent.

Here are some of the final words I wrote:

> *Our planet is gasping and suffering, and we are the only ones who can relieve it. There is purpose enough to do the next most important thing—to make sure that we are each living a mindful, compassionate life. So, what are we*

waiting for? What will you do with the opportunities and challenges that are presented? We now have pictures to illustrate the effects of global warming. Without images, there is no sense of urgency, uproar, or action. The US, which makes up only 4 percent of the population, produces upwards of 25 percent of the world's carbon dioxide. We have about eight more years to reverse the flow of carbon into the atmosphere, or we will soar past the red lines that guard the stability of our ice shelves. This is a social issue unlike anything we have ever faced, and it needs more than a movement. We all need to take responsibility for our thoughts and actions and become part of something bigger than we are—the ultimate calling.

It's hard for me to imagine what in the world I planned to do with myself after writing that last line. I do know that the fire had been burning inside me for more than a decade—a fire to be part of the solution. Like so many people, I was standing on the sidelines, feeling somewhat paralyzed by the enormous task of figuring out what role to play in the fight against climate change. Some call this paralyzis "climate despair."

I do not call myself an activist. Outspoken, yes—I have used my voice for many things over the years, but mostly for inspiration and education. I have read a lot, paid attention to world events, and had the privilege of traveling for a living. I've shared quotes and books that have moved me and have endeavored to find meaning in my life by showing others how much or how little they can control. These words from Austrian philosopher, author, and Holocaust survivor Viktor Frankl come to mind: "Between stimulus and response there is a space. In that space is our power to choose our response. In our response lies our growth and our freedom."

Frankl believed that humans are motivated by something called a "will to meaning"—a desire to find meaning in life. He argued that life can have meaning even in the most miserable of circumstances and that the motivation for living comes from finding that meaning.

I'll never forget my small, red, paperback copy of Wendell Berry's *What Are People For?* In it, he writes about the many revolutions we have been through—agricultural, industrial, technological. He says that slowly, over the years, human beings have almost done away with the need to play an active role in our own survival and livelihoods. For most of us, there's no reason to hunt and gather, no need to raise cattle or tend to crops in order to put food on the table. It is all done for us.

As I write this in 2020, we have seen incredible advances in technology—some so great that many of us cannot keep up. We have expanded the flow and increased the speed of everything. Knowledge, new ideas, medical advice, innovations, insults, rumours, collaboration, commerce, and learning can all circulate globally at unprecedented speed. Almost anyone can plug into these tools and start up a business, receive medical advice, participate in a global debate, or acquire a new skill, from knitting to learning a new language.

All of this vastly amplifies each individual's power. As we have seen, a single person now has more power than ever before, both to construct something positive and to destroy. This power has been taken to negative levels we might wish we had never seen. One example is the 2008 stock market crash. But to focus on the positive: Today, one person can help so many other people! They can entertain and inspire millions of others—as we witnessed first-hand with the amazing singer-songwriter Joss Stone, who joined us on our September 2019 *Hearts in the Ice* send-off for our voyage to Bamsebu. One person is all it takes to share a new idea, story, product, or app with the whole world. With technology at our fingertips, a single person can share with many people at once, and when that happens, we see the power of many.

And, of course, the power of many can be both positive and negative. Human beings as a collective are now not just a part of nature; we have become a *force* of nature. A force that is changing the climate and our ecozystems at a pace and scope never before experienced. But we also have the technology, the tools, and the power to do *good* at a pace and scope never before seen. Today, it's in our power to reverse environmental degradation and to feed, house, and clothe every human being on Earth if we set our collective minds to doing just that.

At the time of this writing, the Covid-19 pandemic has changed everything around the world. Travel is still at a standstill, markets are plunging, people have lost loved ones and jobs, and businesses are shutting down. The call to action could not be clearer: The world needs the power of one to inspire the power of many. From leadership inspiring confidence in a vaccine, to community leaders rebuilding their organizations, to business owners starting anew. Hilde and I have done our fair share of exploring and adventuring in the polar regions, and we have tasted change in both ourselves and the world around us.

On one of my many backpacking trips into the Sierra Nevada Wilderness, I once noticed a wooden sign delineating the entry into the wild with a quote from Henry David Thoreau, etched in golden-yellow ink on the brown wood: "I went to the woods because I wished to live deliberately, to front only the essential facts of life, and see if I could not learn what it had to teach, and not, when I came to die, discover that I had not lived." I yearned to live that quote.

In my twenties, I decided to quit my job as a computer programmer for a bank in Oslo called Manufacturers Hanover (or "Manny Hanny") and join a four-month outdoor leadership school in Canmore, Alberta, called Yamnuska Mountain Adventures. Everyone thought I had lost my mind, leaving my job, the apartment I had recently purchased, and the country I was born in to take up residence in the wilderness with nothing more than a backpack. But I thought it was a brilliant idea. Those four months in my twenties were my entry into ice-climbing, rock climbing, glacier travel, whitewater canoeing, caving, and backcountry skiing. I also fine-tuned my navigation skills and developed leadership skills. If you ever want to really get to know yourself and test your resolve and patience, you should take one of these courses. I was building the foundation I needed if I was to live by Thoreau's words. Over the next decade, my life was all about love, learning, curiosity, taking risks, testing my mettle, making myself humble over and over and over again, and growing into a strong, stoic, proud, confident woman.

My forays into Antarctica started in 1992, before the advent of the internet. I was thirty years old at the time and managing a staff of about fifteen for an outdoor and travel outfitter called Adventure 16. We were based in Solana Beach, California, and I was having the time of my life backpacking in the High Sierra and Joshua Tree National Park, where I taught winter camping, map and compass skills/backcountry navigation, and assisted basic rock climbing. Dirt, trees, the moon, and the stars were my friends. And, of course, my orange '74 Westphalia camper and my buddy John Allen.

Those were the good old days when I formed lasting friendships— friendships that have lived on to this day and which continue to fill my cup with gratitude. I've had so many awesome memories with Deborah Liv,

Teresa, Geoff, Connie, Sandy, Kenji, Johnny, Jeff C., John D., Carol, Mike L., Amber, and so many more.

In 1992, I was selected to be the fourth woman to join the American Women's Expedition to Antarctica (AWE). It felt like I had moved from the minor to the major league almost overnight. This four-woman team aimed to ski the entire length of Antarctica, from ice shelf to ice shelf—a total of 2,400 km (1,500 miles)—over the course of four and a half months. This would be a first—no women had ever even attempted it before. It was a slog across uneven terrain with predominant headwinds, temperatures ranging from -20°C to -32°C (-4°F to -26°F), and each of us pulling a 90 kg (200 lb) sled. There was no rhythm, just hard work planting your pole, pulling your sled, and inhaling, one breath at a time, in the cold, dry Antarctic air. We arrived at the South Pole on January 14, 1993, at 1900 hours—beaten, frostbitten, hungry, tired, and elated. It was -67°C (-89°F). We made history that day! To this day, Ann Bancroft, Sue Giller, Anne Dal Vera, and I toast each other virtually in our own special ways with a sip of whiskey—just like the ol' boys who went to war might have done.

Antarctica has beckoned me often since then. I have been almost a hundred times in total and in a variety of roles: as history lecturer, special guest lecturer, Zodiac driver, education coordinator, and naturalist guide. It's a place beyond taming—you must relinquish the desire to control everything and, instead, let *it* tame *you*. That's why once you've been to Antarctica, you'll never look at things the same way again—and why working in Antarctica can elevate you to your highest potential. A ski expedition across Antarctica forces you to become the best version of yourself. It requires you to step outside of your comfort zone, think and act creatively in order to survive the harsh conditions, and appreciate a simple life. But perhaps most importantly, it requires you to embrace curiosity. And at the end of the day, isn't that what we all want? To allow our inner child a safe space to come out and be curious about everything it finds.

Antarctica and the Arctic: Perhaps it's no great surprise that Hilde and I would be attracted to these polar-opposite places and each to what the other represented. Just as the lines of latitude and longitude converge at the north and south poles, so too did Hilde and me. But our first meeting would be in Alaska in the fall of 2016.

It was the annual Adventure Travel World Summit; I was there repre-senting Polar Latitudes, an Antarctic tour operator, and Hilde was there on behalf of Hurtigruten, a cruise operator that serves the polar regions and all places in between.

Before the conference started, there was a day reserved for fun activities only, when attendees were offered dozens of options for exploring, adventuring, and exercising their bodies or minds. I must have secured one of the last tickets to the conference because there was only one adventure option left for me to choose: an Alaskan glacier cruise. I'll admit that I wasn't thrilled; I paused before making my way to the bus. At this point in my life, I had already taken several ship voyages and seen many glaciers. But in the end, I decided that I didn't want to miss the adventure, so I got on the bus and off we went. I sat next to somebody who introduced himself as Jan Sverre Sivertsen. He was a handsome Norwegian who would soon be starting out on his own epic South Pole adventure. We danced between the English and Norwegian languages, with no shortage of things to share. I was already happy about my decision to get on the bus. Little did I know, that day would alter the course of my life, at least for the next several years.

It was a brisk Alaskan day. The icy air stung our cheeks, and as we cruised toward the glacier's edge, a cup of hot chocolate was a must. And that is exactly where Hilde and I met—next to the hot chocolate. My new friend from the bus, Jan Sverre, knew Hilde and told her a bit about me. There we were side by side filling our mugs with a warm drink. It didn't take long for us both to notice that we were wearing the same ring. *What?* I had never met anyone with the same ring as me, and neither had Hilde. As it turned out, both of our rings were handmade by the same Inuit man from Sisimiut, on the west coast of Greenland. Each of our rings featured the eyes, ears, and nose of a polar bear's head, carved in great detail.

Locating this artist and his carvings had been an adventure in itself— and maybe that's why, in some odd way, it came as no surprise that we had both ended up on the second floor of a warehouse in Sisimiut, on different days and in different years. Isn't that how synchronicity works? Sisimiut seems to have more dogs than people—you can hear them howling everywhere. It feels clean there and free of pollution. The smell of fish permeates the air. The colorful houses are on uneven terrain with dirt slopes. There are no shop signs, so without help from the locals (*turn right at the blue house, left at the yellow house*), it's almost impossible to know where you're going. Finding the warehouse was exciting, and when we got there and opened the door, it was a window into the world of the

Inuit, with paintings and carvings and artefacts on the walls. It was like finding a hidden treasure.

We had so much fun on that boat trip. I met colleagues from Adventure 16 days that I had not seen for years, and I made new lasting friendships. The time with Hilde and the Norwegians on board was a highlight. Hilde was so positive and spirited, as evidenced by the Kvikk Lunsj chocolate and the small bottle of Jägermeister to toast our new friendship. I would come to find out that she always traveled with this small green bottle to toast all of the little and big things along the way. It was one of many parts of her that I came to really appreciate and love. Just one month after Hilde and I met in Alaska, we made plans to meet again. On a crisp autumn day in October, we met at Olivia, a restaurant on the pier by Aker Brygge in Oslo. I had already been planning to visit my father in Norway, so I arranged for Oslo to be my first stop after the long flight from my home in Squamish, British Columbia. It was at Olivia, over mushroom soup and warm sourdough bread, that the seed of an idea about the option of overwintering at Bamsebu was first shared with me. From that day forward, all energy was pointing me north to the Arctic.

A couple of years after that first meeting, in April of 2018, Hilde and I traveled to Bamsebu together for the first time to film clips for our documentary about our planned nine months at Bamsebu. (*Hjerter i isen* aired on January 8, 2021, in Norway for the Norwegian public—half a million people viewed it on its first airing.) In addition to filming, we used the time to explore the logistics of Bamsebu. In particular, we wanted to understand what it might look like if we were to actually overwinter there. Hilde had stayed at Bamsebu many times over a period of more than twenty years, but it was not set up for anything long-term. As we explored, we found ourselves repeating the same phrase to one another: "the power of one." We were beginning to realize the impact the two of us could have by spending nine months living in the same place, collecting data, connecting with youth, and observing the world around us. And that's how our little seed turned into a live project. With this, we embarked on our calling to experience an overwintering alone in the Arctic.

Hilde

To live in Svalbard, immersed by nature, is to meet yourself on an entirely different level. Surrounded by nature bigger than I have ever imagined. Bare tundra, mountain ranges, wide fjords, glaciers as icecaps, and magnificent glacier fronts. The unique wildlife. The Arctic light, midnight sun, and a darkness like none you've ever known. Experiencing the Arctic gives a feeling of being alive like no other place I have experienced. My first encounter with the polar night was filled with both excitement and fear. I admit random, extreme thoughts. *Will I meet a polar bear right here? Am I going to die?* Instead of giving in to the fear, I forced myself to walk alone through the dark nights. I knew that if I gave in to my fear, it would take many possibilities and opportunities away from my life, and I was determined not to allow it to keep me from experiencing Svalbard and its wondrous surroundings.

Darkness. It can be scary! As a child, I was afraid of the dark, of boogie men, I guess, and here I was in the polar night. A night that lasts for three months. It was time to make friends with her, this darkness. Over time, I gained confidence in myself; I learned how to take care of myself and protect myself and to trust in my navigational skills. I learned how to use a flare gun (I knew how to handle a weapon from following my father hunting). There are no boogie men under my bed on Svalbard, but polar bears can be right outside the tent or outside the walls where I sleep. In fact, over the past few decades, I have had more than 300 polar bear encounters. They're just part of the reality of life in Svalbard, and my respect and admiration for these majestic creatures grows with every encounter.

Growing up, I was the youngest of four, and my father's business travels took us all over Europe. That was when I got my first taste of planning for an adventure, the excitement of packing a backpack or a suitcase and hopping on a train. My dear, loving mum and I explored the cities we visited while my dad was in business meetings. My older siblings were home in school. I absolutely loved seeing new places and experiencing new atmospheres and cultures in cities all over Europe like London, Paris, Amsterdam, and Vienna. Tourism was my education, and I continued to travel the world as I became older. Seeing other parts of the world, both on land and at sea, learning about other cultures, languages, and the huge differences in living conditions, poverty, and extreme wealth was an important lesson for me. Later on, I got to experience life underneath the surface of oceans around the world. Scuba diving and diving opened up a whole new world to me! Magical experiences diving at Maldives, Seychelles, Bali, Thailand, South Africa, Caribbean, and Hawaii: The ocean was so full of life! Swimming in an aquarium and learning that sharks were as natural in the environment as the polar bears in the Arctic.

Years later, at Bamsebu, I learned much more about the living organizm the ocean is. The lungs of the earth.

Exploring and doing different activities while traveling to other places became a reason to go. I got to climb and ski mountains, and I had great experiences downhill skiing in the French, Italian, and Austrian Alps. The need to be active has followed me throughout my life. But all the experiences of seeing how other people were living, in conditions so poor I could never imagine, was an eye-opener to me. Experiencing huge differences between living conditions and cultures traveling in Thailand, China, and the Middle East gave me a valuable ballast in life. The people fascinated me, but also the new wildlife I was introduced to. Some encounters were too close and scary, like the terrifying experience waking up with hyenas in the camp looking for food around my tent in Masai Mara in Kenya, or when the car (we were sitting on a roof deck of the car) got stuck in a park in South Africa and an elephant came sniffing on us with his huge trunk while the driver gave us quiet and intense instructions. I had several organized safaris in Africa and South Africa, and yes, it is magical to experience the "big five" or to be in a cage when a big white shark passes a meter away. I was a passionate photographer—on land and in the ocean. All these experiences gave me insights and made me humble and grateful, and I realized how fortunate I was, being born in Norway. But it also taught me that we are all a part of the same world, surrounded by the same air and ocean. Everything on Earth is linked together.

I worked as a travel agent in NSB Reisebyrå (NSB travel bureau) in Oslo, and then, in 1995, I was offered a position with Spitsbergen Travel (now Hurtigruten Svalbard) in Svalbard. This was a huge step for me and changed both my personal life and my career.

Svalbard was so different from anything I'd known in so many ways: the location close to the North Pole, the climate, the wildlife, the small population of less than 1,500 people at that time. It was about 3,000 km (1,864 miles) from my home at Fjellhamar (20 km [12 miles] outside Oslo), and the landscape was completely different from anything I had seen. There were no trees; it was harsh, almost hostile, and the climate was much colder. Instead, there were mountains and glaciers and fjords surrounded by a huge ocean—and, of course, the threat of polar bears. Svalbard is closer to the North Pole than the mainland of Norway, and traveling there from Fjellhamar takes a full day. Driving is not an option since Svalbard is an island. At the time I left, my mum had developed Alzheimer's, but my father urged me to go. I promised myself and my parents I'd visit often, and I did. I visited my parents almost every month for ten years, and they had several trips up to me until they both died in 2005.

When I moved to Svalbard, it felt like coming home. The place enveloped me in so many ways, and I never looked back. Since then, Svalbard has come to define me more than any other place or time in life. I met Steinar two months after I arrived in Longyearbyen. A whole new journey began. Steinar was a widower with two young kids: Frode, twelve years, and Susanne, ten years. I had a new job at a new and unfamiliar place and a new family. Quite overwhelming. Steinar became my new foundation in life, and his children became like my own children. It felt like a huge responsibility but building my own family and supporting Steinar in his parenthood was an exciting, defining, and demanding time for which I was, and remain still, very grateful. I love being a part of Frode and Susanne's lives and seeing them grow up. Now, I'm a grandmother to William, Vilde, and Mia!

Through decades of expeditions, both alone or with Steinar or friends, I have learned about myself and my strengths, weaknesses, and capabilities. The place has tested my limits, both physically and mentally. The wilderness has been a great teacher to me and has filled me with the longing to explore more, to fulfillll my dreams and my curiosity.

Then came the day of reckoning.

First, I had the sensation of being watched. Was that a movement behind me? I turned around and a silent gasp climbed up through my chest. Sudden as a puff of frozen breath, there she was: a massive polar bear, less than 15 meters (50 feet) away. She had snuck up behind me while I was fiddling with my new film camera. I was actually filming a large male polar bear hunting on the sea ice a few hundred meters away. I stayed on my knees, completely still, and looked her right in the eyes. Oh, I felt so very small. So very, very small. Would she attack? Would I manage to get to the door on the other side of the hut? I have seen how quickly they move during a hunt or an approach. Would I be able to reach for my revolver, open up the Velcro on my holster, grab the weapon, and fire the gun to protect myself? I kept a calm resolve. I knew the answers, but this could go very wrong, very quickly. Even though my heart was pumping madly, I felt a sort of peacefulness wash over me.

She was absolutely stunning, awe-inspiring, with the sunset behind her, making her fur glow pink and purple. Without taking my eyes off her, I slowly angled the lens of the camera that was hanging around my neck, pointed it in her direction, and took a few pictures. I had no idea if she was in the frame. Seconds felt like minutes. She lifted her left paw, and I thought, *Okay, now I am in deep trouble.* I wouldn't even be able to blink before she was all over me. Then I remembered Nikita—who has more experience in polar bear behavior than almost anyone else, having experienced more than 2,000 polar bear encounters at Wrangel Island—once telling me, "Stand your ground, Hilde. And no vocals. Animals scream in distress."

I didn't make a sound. I just kept staring at her. In a strange way, I felt confident. She placed the lifted paw slowly and gently in front of her, and with one step, she turned her whole body facing the sea ice to a 90-degree angle and slowly started to walk. She kept looking at me while she walked away. After walking a few meters, she found a rock, maybe a meter (three feet) high and wide, and lay down behind it. The rock wasn't big enough to hide all of her—her head would poke out over it, then she'd hide again. Was she playing hide and seek with me? Some sort of playful hunt? After a minute or two, she began to walk out onto the ice toward the big male.

Moving to Svalbard meant embracing encounters like this and leaving behind the secure and familiar terrain of home. Until then, I had lived in a safe environment, full of family and friends, but I left it all to explore this remote outpost of the world. Svalbard is listed as "one of the world's last wildernesses" and one of its northernmost inhabited areas, but to me, it was simply beautiful. Home. Much of the work in Svalbard revolved around mining, science, research, travel, and tourism. Working in the travel industry, I really wanted the guests to experience and see Svalbard the way I did. To feel what I felt. To go home having had a life-changing experience. To become polar ambassadors.

As a tour operator on land and at sea, we knew we had a huge responsibility for the environment, and our goal was to "leave no footprint, take nothing but pictures." Focus on the vulnerable landscape, wildlife, and protected areas and sites. Don't step on flowers, keep your distance from protected cultural heritage, and don't disturb any wildlife. The history of

Svalbard is so full of adventure and early explorers. In retrospect, I think we could have had even more to share if we had closer dialogue with our neighbors in Longyearbyen—the scientists-at the University Center in Svalbard (UNIS) and the Norwegian Polar Institute.

It was life in the outdoors that really beckoned and tested me. This was a place where stories of true survival were born, and I wanted to taste that in its fullness. I realized that what I wanted most of all was to overwinter—to experience being in nature through a full winter season, the changes in light, the wildlife, completely immersed in nature and nothing else.

In the early 2000s, it became clear that things were changing in Svalbard. We were experiencing warmer temperatures, more grass, less sea ice, and more precipitation than normal. The rain that now came more frequently in the winter froze to ice on the tundra and the snow; as the permafrost melted during summer, in addition to more rain, landslides occurred. These changes were accumulating year after year; it was worrisome.

Then, one Saturday morning, December 19, 2015, a huge avalanche in the heart of Longyearbyen swept eleven of my neighbors' houses away. Houses, cars, and snowmobiles were all crushed and buried under tons of snow. Everybody in the town began to dig and do anything they could to help locate survivors. The tragedy cost two lives—two people killed while they sat inside their homes. I was involved in helping the family who lost a two-year-old daughter. I will never forget that day. It was devastating and surreal, and it stirred up very difficult emotions, reminding us of nature's brutality. All of our lives were forever changed.

About a year after the avalanche, I met Sunniva in Alaska. I was so inspired by her experiences and felt an instant connection. We connected through our experiences and our shared interest in exploration. We had both experienced the extreme and vulnerable nature at the poles and the changes taking place there. We spoke about the beauty and the wildlife of these regions and our experiences of them, about the importance of sustainability and climate-change mitigation, and about our desire to experience the true powers of Mother Nature. Immediately, I felt like I had met a soul sister. There was no doubt in my mind that I would ask her if she would be interested in joining me for an overwintering. Sunniva came to Svalbard in December of the same year, and we had a short ski expedition to experience the polar night, Sunniva's first experience of the total darkness. I had no doubt that we, as the first two women in history, would manage to undertake the challenge an overwintering would entail. We had the physical and mental strength, the stamina, and the determination we needed for a challenge like this. And that's how it all began: our plans for the overwintering and the first phase of *Hearts in the Ice*.

Here in the Arctic, only a small number of life forms can survive. All life is pushed to the limit. It is inhospitable, cold, and barren. There is little nourishment to be found for much of the year. The growing season is short for both plants, insects, and animals. Flowers struggle to emerge from the permafrost when the upper layer melts in the summer, and the birds have to work hard to feed themselves and their chicks, who have just a brief spell to fledge. This is life lived outside of what seems possible. But even so, there are species that belong up here: polar bears, arctic foxes, reindeer adapted over the course of millions of years, and ptarmigans. And people like me: I feel that I belong up here too. I feel strong when the weather whips around me, when I sense that I am part of something bigger than myself—when the forces are raging, and I know how to protect myself. I've never felt as strong as I do in these situations. But to reach that place, to gather that experience and confidence, I've needed to push my limits for the past twenty-five years. Many times, I've felt small, afraid, and vulnerable. Here in the Arctic, you have to work for your existence, whether man, woman, or beast.

"Mother Nature needs her daughters"—this was the call to action raised by an organization called Homeward Bound, with the goal of inspiring women in STEMM to take on leadership roles in the climate crisis. We both decided that we would answer that call via *Hearts in the Ice*, whose name itself speaks to our shared love of the polar regions.

The idea of overwintering at Bamsebu was Hilde's love for and fascination with the landscape, wildlife, ice, and snow, as well as the magical Arctic light experienced through her deep, immersive exploration here—a place most people have never even seen. Our project, *Hearts in the Ice*, was the blend of this unique opportunity to overwinter for nine months and the possibility to have it be a platform for global dialogue around climate change. We decided to use this platform to be leaders and serve as a bridge between researchers, school children, and citizens in response to climate change. We were the collaborators, and we used our words, images, video, and research to paint a picture of what is happening in the Arctic. We didn't just love this region; we also wanted to protect what we loved so dearly. Our time at Bamsebu has given us an otherworldly adventure to share with you; our isolation experience is a story we hope will live beyond our years. We made history as the first two women to overwinter solo through Svalbard's harsh polar night—but we didn't do it alone.

During our stay at Bamsebu, we were able to align with world-renowned researchers from Scripps Institution of Oceanography, NASA, the Norwegian Polar Institute (NPI), the University Center in Svalbard (UNIS), and the British Columbia Institute of Technology (BCIT). We are "citizen scientists," participating and collaborating in scientific research used to increase knowledge of our planet and the massive changes it is experiencing.

Børge Damsgård, one of our research partners from UNIS, shared the following about the importance of citizen science and our time at Bamsebu:

> One challenge we face is that most people do not feel connected to the huge efforts in data collection going on all over the world. They are thus not motivated to interpret large-scale changes that, simply put, will decide not only the fate of polar nature, but presumably the existence of the world as we know it. Citizen science is a way to close the gap between people perceiving the world around them and the scientists monitoring changes in the climate. As such, the Bamsebu project has a very important added value in its long-term educational potential.

This public participation in scientific research allowed us to feel a sense of connection to the world during our time at Bamsebu. All of the data we collected has been conveyed to our research partners for analyzis. By collecting samples over such an extended period, we are contributing to the huge global data collection as Damsgård mentions above. As we experience shifts in everything from attitudes to sustainability to leadership, empowering citizens to understand that their observations and contributions are needed and valuable can have a major impact on our world. Being citizen scientists allows us to participate in the conversations that scientists are having about climate and our delicate ecozystem. And let's face it, science points to this decade that we are in as the defining one, a tipping point that affects all of us.

Through *Hearts in the Ice*, we have realized a dream, and we want to continue to inspire others, especially women and children, to pursue their dreams. We hope the stories we share in the chapters to come will inspire action. Through our own research and adventures, we want to promote public engagement with science so that you, dear reader, can assess your own relationship with science and your curiosity. You will see that you don't have to be a data analyzt or a biology graduate to help improve conditions on our planet. All you have to do is allow yourself the space to connect to the natural world and remain curious about your role in it and how you can expand upon that role. You can take steps to protect our planet in your everyday life.

In this book, we will share what we call our "Bamsebu Blueprint"—key learnings we've gathered on our journey, which made it possible for us to survive and thrive during our year at Bamsebu. We'll share:

- Tips on coping with isolation
- How to deal with fear and uncertainty
- Tricks for managing in small spaces
- How to deal with stress through routine and self-care
- How to live with a smaller footprint
- How to maximize the use of food while minimizing waste
- How to appreciate silence and nature
- How to navigate the dark spaces outside and inside our minds
- The value and power of collaboration

Most importantly, these lessons will reveal why each one of us must engage in the climate conversation and how curiosity can help us all find purpose. We hope our blueprint can serve as a roadmap not just for your own survival but for thriving in a rapidly changing world.

CHAPTER 1

WE PROTECT WHAT WE LOVE

A GLOBAL VIEW

Never doubt that a small group of thoughtful, committed citizens
can change the world. Indeed, it is the only thing that ever has.
— Margaret Mead

SUNNIVA

Like most everyone else in North America, I was glued to the TV on the night of November 8, 2016. The race to the White House was on; the electoral results poured in. By the end of the night, the new president would be named. It seemed infinitely clear to me, and everyone I knew, that Hillary Clinton would whip her opponent's ass.

She would have big shoes to fill, with the outgoing articulate, charismatic Barack Obama leaving the desk. I remember going to bed more excited than I'd been in years. Excited that I would wake up to the country's first female president. Excited to go to my first inauguration with my sister, Bettina. I had tickets and had reserved our hotel in Washington,

DC—we were to arrive on January 19, 2017, and were eager to celebrate Hillary's win.

Instead, we would use that visit to participate in the March on Washington—a march against everything the new president stood for. When the time came, Bettina was too busy with work and couldn't take part. I was disappointed, but to my surprise and delight, my new friend Hilde was super game to join me for the march. So, I flew from Vancouver International Airport in British Columbia, she flew from the Oslo Airport, and we met in Washington, DC.

With our Canadian and Norwegian flags in tow, we explored the city on foot and by bicycle. Not only did Hilde and I share an appreciation for the great outdoors and protecting our planet, but we were also now bound by a shared love for equality and the human spirit. We both felt compelled to show up, lend our voices in unity, and try to understand how in the world the country had voted this man into office.

I knew only four people at the march: Debbie Harrell and her daughter, Maddie—family friends from Catalina Island—and Jody Sims and her partner, Suzanne, who flew in from Texas. Jody is the founder and publisher of the *Women's Times* in San Diego and had done a feature on me and the South Pole expedition back in 1994. That was when I was introduced to Gloria Steinem, the feminist, activist, and women's rights leader. I had just returned from the South Pole, and I was so green and naive about the world that I didn't fully appreciate the depth of who she was. Even so, I remember her being so gracious and full of compliments about what we had done for women and Antarctica—how we had broken the ice ceiling.

We ran all around Washington. We met Jody and Suzanne at the hotel, and they gave us the lowdown on where to go, who would be speaking, and how to get there. There were hundreds of thousands of people criss-crossing the city.

I will never forget the energy of that day.

This was no "ordinary" anything. People were dancing, chanting, and walking with kids on their shoulders; they had their faces painted every which color and were dressed up, holding hand-painted signs bearing slogans of peace and love. Strangers smiled at you, hugged you, danced with you . . . it was electric, and we felt so alive and free. That day is forever etched in my mind—a symbol of what it looks like when humans come together in spirit, aligned around protecting the most precious thing: each other. We hopped up on a pile of barricades and listened to Gloria

Steinem's speech: she's ageless and was as mobilizing and electric as ever. Both Hilde and I were moved to tears as strangers came up to hug us and thank us for showing up—because it was the showing up that mattered. It all made me realize I had spent years as a silent advocate on issues I cared about. I made a promise that day to no longer be silent. I vowed to myself, and to society, that I would always try to show up, physically and vocally.

After our time together in DC, Hilde was not only a dear friend, she had become a sister in arms: somebody who also cared deeply about standing up and speaking out. It was a long weekend and a whirlwind trip for both of us, but it served to anchor our connection and our mutual interests—the things we were both passionate about. Little did we know back then that in just three short years, we would be standing up for Mother Nature and her human-driven woes.

Fast-forward to 2019, when we left for Bamsebu and our nine-month overwintering. The world had seen such a rapid escalation in those three years—so much change, destruction, and habitat loss, and so many lives lost through earthquakes, forest fires, hurricanes . . . destruction on a scale that could be a book in itself, so I won't try to sum it up here. Suffice to say that those years proved beyond a doubt that we are at a tipping point as the earth and all its species, including humans, rotate on an axis wobbling further and further off-center. We don't have a choice anymore: We need to recalibrate our compasses. If we are going to make any changes in this world—whether in relation to climate change or to racism, sexism, ageism, or any other form of discrimination—we must each model the changes we wish to see. For Hilde and me, that meant combining the quarter centuries we had each spent in devotion to the polar regions to create the project that is *Hearts in the Ice*.

Travel does many things to a person. I do not think of our world as having borders. Having traveled to the extreme north and south and numerous places in between, I have collected stories and images along the way. But most importantly, I have seen how several cultures can be born into one small place—and thrive. I have observed just a fraction of the many ways we can live together in this world. This has shown me that borders don't exist.

Years ago, I was introduced to a citizen-science program onboard the Expedition cruise ship Hebridean Sky. The program was operated by my then-employer, Polar Latitudes, and pioneered in earnest by veteran polar guides Bob Gilmore and Annette Bombosch in Antarctica. It was an instant hit. Regular people with an interest in science were taken, step-by-step, through projects that explored cloud observation, Southern Ocean temperature changes, species distribution, wildlife sightings, saltwater collection, and phytoplankton sampling. These types of community-science programs are especially helpful in remote and difficult destinations like Antarctica and the Arctic—hotspots of climate change.

Engaging nonscientists highlights that if we want to better understand changes in biodiversity and the climate as well as what individuals can do about it, it's important to collaborate. It is an unintimidating way for *anyone* to stay passionately curious about changes only scientists would typically observe. Creating transparency around data collection allows nonscientists to apply their own thinking to make sense of findings and interpret data in a new way—one that isn't clouded by too many technicalities. This can open the door for scientists to see things from a new angle, and, in turn, helps nonscientists begin to really value their research, leading, perhaps, to investing more time and care in future citizen-science projects by encouraging their friends and family, for instance, to join in or becoming ambassadors to the places they travel to. Participating in data collection helps citizen scientists feel invested in not just the journey to find answers but also the actions needed to make a realiztic change. They're not being told what to do anymore—they understand what to do and why and will be more likely to follow through with it.

Taking part in active and relevant projects as citizen scientists was the most natural fit for *Hearts in the Ice*; it was also our way of keeping the promise we made on inauguration day, to stand up for the causes we cared about. We would get involved, speak up for what we loved, and at the same time, work to protect those things we loved. Being citizen scientists would allow us to explore and highlight the changes in the world, then engage in constructive action.

Stories connect us, and it's through stories that we've come to understand the importance and timing of our projects and data collection. Hilde and I faced a learning curve as we tried to understand which projects would make the most impact, which ones we could reasonably agree to, and which would also be of most interest to the scientists. Learning to make these decisions took a full year of research and listening to stories, but the more we read and listened, the clearer our plan became.

There were two science stories that really caught our attention early on, both relating to things we can't normally see day-to-day: fulmars and phytoplankton. Fulmars are pelagic seabirds that belong to the large group of the tubenoses (Procellariiformes), of which albatrosses are the best-known representatives. These birds forage exclusively at sea and are rarely seen close to shore. The fulmar is a poor diver and thus feeds on what's available at or within a few meters of the water's surface. Like most tube-nosed seabirds, fulmars regularly ingest a variety of marine debris, most of it probably eaten directly, either intentionally because it resembles prey or unintentionally when mixed with attractive food wastes (since nearly everything that floats in the ocean gains a coating that smells like their food source—and often, it's microplastics). They also ingest debris indirectly, for instance, through fish or scavenging on the guts of other dead animals.

The details of the sizes ingested need to be assessed, but a preliminary survey suggested that roughly 90 percent of ingested plastic items (not threads or soft sheets) found in the first glandular stomach of fulmars measures 10 mm (0.4 inches) or less in size, and more than 50 percent measures 5 mm (0.2 inches) or less (Bravo Rebolledo 2011).[1] So what's the sad fact about this? These birds become unable to digest food and die of starvation . . . because they are eating plastic waste. They die of starvation because they eat plastic.

In a study conducted ten years ago, one in ten dead fulmars had ingested plastic in their stomach lining. Today, nine out of ten dead fulmars are found with plastic in their stomach lining!

The amount of plastic these birds are ingesting reflects the insane abundance of litter in our environment. Now take that a step further: This is just one species of bird studied; imagine how many other birds, or animals, are eating trash Every. Single. Day. You don't need to be a scientist to grasp the destruction that plastic (and waste in general) wreaks on most animals out there—both the ones we see and the ones we don't. As citizen scientists, after reviewing the data above, we can understand the impact of plastic waste and decide which actions we need to take to reduce this impact.

Then there are phytoplankton—microscopic drifting plants. Researchers are not entirely sure how the microscopic world responds to melting glaciers or during the long polar winters. Phytoplankton use sunlight to make energy and organic carbon that provide food (primary

---

[1] Elisa L. Bravo Rebolledo, "Threshold levels and size-dependent passage of plastic litter in stomachs of Fulmars" (MSc thesis, Wageningen University, Department of Aquatic Ecology and Water Quality Management, 2011), 32pp.

production) for other animals. These primary producers play a critical role in drawing carbon dioxide out of the atmosphere and generate more than half of the world's oxygen! That's more than the trees and plants on land combined. This was big news to us, and after talking to several people interested in these tiny plants, we found FjordPhyto, a citizen-science project started by Allison Cusick of Scripps Institution of Oceanography. Fjord Phyto brings together polar travelers and scientists in an effort to understand the changes in marine ecozystems. We became instant fans. Allison made it super easy to understand the dynamic chain of events that threatens phytoplankton production—and she was most likeable too.

The bottom line: Phytoplankton are key to life. As you may have guessed, since they're so critical to our world's oxygen, their existence (and, in turn, nonexistence) has a huge effect on our environment and civilization. They sit at the base of the marine food web, and their distribution and abundance change throughout the season, but also with the changing climate. As we learned about these itty-bitty things, our curiosity grew. These are things we can barely see (though water clarity and phytoplankton abundance can be measured using a Secchi disk), yet as we read about them, we were ever more aware of their enormous power. These microscopic plankton have the power to change the lives of all of the species we *can* see out there. They could literally make or break every ecozystem on Earth, especially that of our ocean.

Clearly, it's important to learn more about these organizms. One way to do that is by sampling them frequently throughout the season to get an understanding of which types of phytoplankton are present and how they change from month to month. However, as Hilde and I learned through the people we talked to and the stories we researched, this is something few scientists have the funding, resources, or time to accomplish.

We, however, were able to collect phytoplankton throughout our Arctic winter at Bamsebu. By collecting samples over time, we have been able to help build a greater dataset to allow scientists to understand how melting glaciers influence phytoplankton. It was a lot of work and organization, but so much fun!

Speaking of glaciers—now's a good time to mention that multiyear sea ice is disappearing and will be replaced by first-year sea ice, which will cause shifts in ice algal communities, with cascading effects on the ice-associated ecozystem.

- Seasonal duration of first-year sea ice is expected to become shorter, with more snow on the ice, which may decrease the growth season for ice algae, with unknown consequences for biodiversity.
- Sea ice is an important Arctic habitat that supports a rich diversity of species—many of which we still know little about.
- It is possible that the structure of the sea-ice algal community has changed in the central Arctic between the 1980s and 2010s. This change probably occurred when sea ice extent and thickness declined, but also when sampling efforts and regions shifted, so it is difficult to attribute change.
- Ice amphipod abundance has declined around Svalbard since the 1980s, coinciding with declining sea-ice conditions.
- Changes in sea-ice biota are very challenging to detect because sea ice is a dynamic system with large natural variability, and there has been a lack of consistent sea-ice biota monitoring.
- Sea-ice biota are affected by temperature and salinity, nutrient and space limitations, and the ephemeral nature of the ice habitat, therefore making them very susceptible to climate change.
- Sea-ice biota monitoring has occurred most frequently in the central Arctic, Svalbard, Utqiaġvik (Alaska), and the Canadian Arctic, with new sites developing in Greenland.

We hope you reach the same conclusions we did after learning about the fulmar and plastic waste and the purpose of phytoplankton: It's time to roll up our sleeves and give these microscopic things more visibility. This is a time to question what we value as people. If we value life, then we must work on preserving our earth, and we must—we absolutely must—take gentle care of ourselves and each other. Be kind. Respect our differences. Embrace the diversity all of life represents. Look at others as teachers of something we need to learn or understand.

You may wonder what this has to do with reducing plastic or helping phytoplankton survive, but we believe it has everything to do with it. When you begin to care about others—including people you've never met—you feel a sense of ownership of this world and your choices in it. When you realize that taking care of yourself allows you to love those around you, you begin to see yourself as part of the bigger picture—that is, your actions have a ripple effect.

HILDE

Over the last fifteen years, in particular, we've seen jarring changes in the Arctic, including the impacts of the melting glaciers. When I came to Svalbard in 1995, it was an "Arctic desert," so-called because it was barren and desolate, with less precipitation than the Sahara Desert. The only green grass in Longyearbyen (the largest settlement in Svalbard, with approximately 2,400 inhabitants in 2020) was behind the old "cowshed" and alongside the sewage leak from the houses at Blåmyra. But this is no longer the case, and as the temperature continues to shift, it presents a new set of changes and challenges. In the summer, the warmer climate has turned Svalbard green. I saw all these changes without asking too many questions. Around the time I arrived at Longyearbyen, the scientists were looking at what type of grass could grow in Svalbard, trying out a lot of different sorts without succeeding. But slowly, the whole island turned more and more green with every passing summer. Now there is grass everywhere.

Don't get me wrong, it's nice to look at, but it signifies an obvious change. We have learned that some animals really benefit: Those that nourish themselves by grazing on the tundra—reindeer, grouse, migratory birds, and foxes—are climate *winners* in this round. But when we get to the winter, the same reindeer now struggle with the over-icing on the tundra.[2] It is almost impenetrable and difficult for the reindeer to scrape through to access food. They try to find sustenance wherever they can—often eating kelp and seaweed that they find on the coast.

In 1998, the sea ice formed naturally, and I drove my snowmobile to the neighboring settlements of Pyramiden and Barentsburg, both popular tourist attractions, then across the entire open Isfjorden, northward to the settlement of Ny-Ålesund. The sea ice was more than 40 kms (25 miles) across. I did the same thing in 2004 and again in 2008, but that was the last winter that saw ice in the fjords like this. These days, the ice in the fjords has shrunk to the inner part of the fjord. Less ice in the fjords creates problems for seals, who give birth to their young in caves formed in "pockets" in the ice, and the polar bears that feed on seals lying on the ice. Fast-forward to our winter at Bamsebu, when we observed polar

---

[2] Brage Bremset Hansen, Jon Runar Lorentzen, Jeffrey M. Welker, Øystein Varpe, Ronny Aanes, Larissa Beumer, and Åshild Ønvik Pedersen, "Reindeer turning maritime: Ice-locked tundra triggers changes in dietary niche utilization," *Ecosphere* (April 2019).

bears hunting reindeer. This might be an example of the polar bear trying to adapt to the changing conditions: Diminishing sea ice means fewer available seals, so the polar bears are forced to try and sustain themselves on land animals like reindeer. Their primary food source seems to become less and less available. They are all trying to adapt, but will they succeed? The sea ice has probably an even greater meaning, besides what we can see, to all life in the ocean, as we have come to understand.

The unanticipated consequences of changes in life under the sea ice are one reason we wanted to collect data for research scientists. So far, researchers know that sea ice is important for the first stages of a great many sea organizms' lives and that it's an important link in the whole food chain. Unfortunately, we may not be able to determine just how important before the sea ice is gone for good.

Janne Søreide from the University Center in Svalbard (UNIS), based in Longyearbyen, says, "We know nearly nothing about the consequences of less sea ice for the thousands of microscopic animals that live inside the sea ice. Researchers see that the sea ice in coastal areas can be a very important growth medium for the initial larval stage of many Arctic benthos."[3]

I had learned of Janne and her colleagues Børge Damsgård and Kim Holmén many years before Sunniva and I spent our season at Bamsebu. The UNIS building, where the Norwegian Polar Institute has its main office, is the biggest building in our little settlement, and many of my friends work there or have studied there. Longyearbyen is a small settlement founded in 1906 by the American John Munro Longyear. (Ten years later, he sold the settlement to a Norwegian coal company, who named their new home Longyearbyen—"Longyear Town" in Norwegian). For decades, Longyearbyen was a company town. Its sole purpose was to support the mining operation and provide homes and services for the employees and families. A dilemma with living in Longyearbyen, though, was that the coal mines emitted ten times more CO_2 to the atmosphere than on the mainland of Norway! These days, although coal mining still exists, there's more to the local economy. Tourism, education, science and research factor large. It's a very tight-knit community, so it's natural to meet researchers while having coffee, training at the gym, or just going to the store.

---

[3] Janne Søreide, Eva Leu, Jørgen Berge, Martin Graeve, and Stig Falk-Pettersen, "Timing of blooms, algal food quality, and Calanus glacialis reproduction and growth in a changing Arctic," Global Change Biology (January 2010).

At Bamsebu, we took regular ice-core samples so that the researchers could find out more about what lives in the ice. "Ice algae—algae that lives inside the ice—is considered a very important link in the marine food chain, and it is possible that these small animals that we don't know much about are similarly important,"[4] says Søreide.

Changing temperatures create a domino effect. Disappearing sea ice and snowcaps on glaciers makes a difference. So, what happens when there are fewer "white" surfaces? To answer that question, it's only right to turn to the expert, the international director of the Norwegian Polar Institute, Kim Holmén. He says:

> One important cause of so-called Arctic amplification (accelerating temperature increase) is that less snow means less reflection of sunlight. Darker surfaces and an ice-free sea absorb the heat from the sun. Consequently, the sun heats more in the spring and summer and intensifies the warming . . . we have had 110 months in a row with above-average temperatures. And the trend points upward.[5]

In short: when dark sea and tundra replace snow and ice, the temperature intensifies. It's as though Earth puts on a black T-shirt instead of a white one. Higher temperatures also lead to changes that aren't so easy to see. For instance, permafrost melts, causing unstable foundations for buildings and, as we have seen, can also cause landslides. Permafrost also holds large reserves of methane in the Arctic tundra. Years ago, we never worried about the permafrost melting since, as the word itself implies, it should be permanently frozen. But as Kim Holmén shared in an email exchange with us:

> Methane in and of itself is not dangerous to life in the concentrations we're talking about that are released from melted tundra, but methane is a powerful greenhouse gas . . . Methane also affects the atmosphere's chemical characteristics and contributes to the development of smog.

---

[4] Ibid.

[5] Shukman, David. "Arctic Ice Melting at 'Amazing' Speed, Scientists Find," September 7, 2012. https://www.bbc.com/news/world-europe-19508906.

There are large amounts of carbon stored as methane in the permafrost. Each methane molecule contains a carbon atom. The amount of carbon stored in the form of methane and methane hydrate (which is found both on land in permafrost and in the sea at depths of 200 meters [650 feet]) is at least as large as the amount of all fossil fuels in the word. To be defined as a fossil fuel, like coal, gas, or oil, it must be economically profitable. In other words, there is much more of these materials in the tundra than in the known reserves of coal, gas, and oil. If the permafrost melts and all the methane is released, we're talking about completely incomprehensible changes in the atmosphere.

When we read this, we just want to cry about the brutality of this truth.

When I asked Kim if I may claim, with scientific accuracy, that the world, my world, our world, is "out of balance," the calm, good-natured Swedish expert replied:

"Out of balance" can mean different things to different people. What we can say is that we have greater changes now than we have seen in modern memory. Nature is continuously trying to rebalance itself, and the new balance will be very different than the one we are used to and the one we have organized society to function in. The new balance will be impossible for many animals and organizms to adapt to.

Kim's response leaves me with an even clearer understanding that this is an extremely serious situation. We see and hear about it every single day. Life in nature is being extinguished: organizms, insects, animals, our entire ecozystem. To live in a place like Svalbard gives you an opportunity to become one with the elements—with the mountains, the land, the rocks, the wildlife, the water, and all the microscopic things that connect one to the other. If you look to your right, you might see a receding glacier and think it's just a part of the normal cycle. If you look to your left, you might see rain freezing the tundra and the reindeer struggling to scrape through and think it's just a bad year with random warming. But living among these trends, and with science and scientists tracking them, we cannot escape them. The trends are real, and every year I've been here, I have experienced greater changes.

We have stretched our elastic band so far that it seems to be hard to snap back to its original shape, and I do also wonder how resilient and adaptable we will find ourselves to be.

Even though there's no way to prove that it was a consequence of climate change, the avalanche in Longyearbyen that destroyed eleven neighboring houses and cost two human lives in 2015 was an unprecedented occurrence, certainly in terms of its scale and tragedy. Personally, I feel that it was just the first sign that the powers of nature are frighteningly out of balance.

According to Kim, even if we were to stop all emissions now, the ripple effects of what we do today will be with us for three decades. This should tell us that it is time to take control of our lives, our reactions, and our resources—now.

But it's not all doom and gloom, and it might not be too late to stop this negative cycle. I asked Kim: Is there any good news? Here's what he said:

> Awareness and discussions around climate and the environment are much more serious today than they were forty years ago. And most people have at least some knowledge and thoughts about what they can and perhaps will do. The coronavirus is not good news, but society's response shows that we can make large, rapid changes. It's important to get people to understand that the climate and environment are just as important as your own life now. Because this has to do with the lives of our children and grandchildren. It's just as important as our own lives [were] in 2020.

In other words: We are capable of changing, if we really want to or feel that we have to. The reduction in emissions we saw during the pandemic crisis gave Mother Earth and every living being a breather. The Global Carbon Project reported that "fossil CO_2 emissions have fallen in all the world's biggest emitters [. . .] including by 12% in the US, 11% in the EU, 9% in India and 1.7% in China."

It truly makes a difference when everyone helps out and does their part and when everyone takes responsibility. Because, as human beings, we take care of what we love.

Hearts in the Ice is our way of doing just that. Through this project, we are highlighting all the changes, big and small, that we can make as individuals to create change. Protecting this fragile land and creating awareness around it by engaging people comes naturally to us because we live by one rule: We protect what we love. If everyone takes this approach, engaging with what they love day in and day out, positive change will come naturally.

CHAPTER 2

HJERTER I ISEN

Hearts in the Ice

Be patient toward all that is unsolved in your heart and try to love the questions themselves, like locked rooms and like books that are now written in a very foreign tongue. Do not now seek the answers, which cannot be given you because you would not be able to live them. And the point is, to live everything. Live the questions now. Perhaps you will then gradually, without noticing it, live along some distant day into the answer.
— Rainer Maria Rilke

Hearts in the Ice had been percolating inside each of us for many, many years. A series of choices we each made sent us on our own separate journeys, and through one chance meeting in Alaska, those journeys converged into one. From taking an interest in the outdoors at an early age to carefully watching the changing climate, we have both developed a deep passion for our world and the people in it. Each step in our individual journeys may have seemed random at the time (like both buying a custom-made polar bear ring from a small-town jewelry carver), but those steps were, in fact, stitches, weaving together the growing tapestry of our shared fates and *Hearts in the Ice*.

SUNNIVA

If you were to come upon an old scrapbook from my childhood, you would find a black-and-white picture with jagged edges, showing my mom in an elegant classic suit with four towheaded kids lined up next to her, standing on a pier in Rotterdam with a ship in the background. We were each a year apart, starting with Martin as the oldest, then Kris, myself, and Bettina—the best for last.

That photo is etched in my mind as an icon of my upbringing and the years that followed. My dad was the captain of an oil tanker, so we moved a lot; my mom raised us mostly solo, and ships and the open sea figured prominently. In that photo, Bettina is holding a doll, and I'm holding a suitcase. Today, Bettina has a son, Kjell Ensign, and I suppose I am still moving around with a suitcase in one hand.

My parents immigrated to Canada from Norway when I was just a year old—first stop, Halifax, Nova Scotia. If Canada is the country that mostly shaped me, Norway is the one that defined many of my values and always calls me back, and the US is the one that edged me out of my comfort zone, encouraged me to live without boundaries, and added fuel to my dreams of learning to survive and thrive in the outdoors.

At the age of twenty-eight, I was driving north on Highway 395 in California, heading toward the Sierra Nevada with my friend Steven Carre. I had one hand in a bag of Cheetos and the other hand on the steering wheel. With a long drive ahead of us, Steven decided to ask me what my hundred goals or dreams were. It must have been something he read in a book—but wherever he got it from, *why not?* One by one, my list was formed. I still have that piece of paper. One of my goals was to write a book and, well, here it is! Another was to meet the Dalai Lama and Meryl Streep—these goals have not been met . . . yet. Another was to live in Norway for a year. And here I am, having lived as a resident of Svalbard for the past year. Bamsebu has been my home for the past year, and it's the only place where I can be surrounded by the things that now define me. It's all here at Boulevard Bamsebu—parts of my past, present, and future, all within 20 square meters (215 square feet) of space.

Always a risk-taker, I have moved more times and had more jobs than I can count. At job interviews, I would often be asked, "What is it about this job that makes you think you'll want to stay?" And I have always managed to answer with honesty and sincerity, "I believe I am exactly where I am supposed to be." At every given moment, the job I've had has been the perfect one.

When my former high school held its annual career day for senior girls one year, I was invited to share my life and career choices with the girls. I read through the list of other women who were going to speak at the event and immediately felt a bit . . . how should I say? . . . underqualified. This prompted me to evaluate my experiences, going over all the skills and knowledge I had amassed from my various jobs and the teams I had worked with. I realized I had learned a lot! It reminded me of something the American systems philosopher Buckminster Fuller said: "The specialist bird is greatly impeded by its wings when trying to walk." I always took this to mean that we are living in a time when it's important to develop multiple skills sets, and that we should endeavor to build our emotional intelligence and our intellect. When I looked at it that way, I did have a lot to offer.

Though I've often been called a risk-taker, I haven't always thought of myself as one. This might prompt the question: *Well then, Sunniva, what are you? Why do you make the decisions you make?* I believe that my interest in working such varied jobs and traveling when and where I felt was right came from curiosity. I have always been so intrigued by human potential and by what makes us tick and why.

This curiosity was kindled at a very early age when I would wonder where my father went for so many months at a time. Though he was a man of routine—for breakfast, he'd always have oatmeal and a spoonful of cod liver oil, which we all thought was so gross—as an oil-tanker captain, he was away often. To me, his time away was always represented by postcards from the edge, portraying either exotic destinations or shipping ports that all looked alike. When he came back, we always got Twist candies and gifts.

My parents were also very driven. When my father came back from sea, he would always grill us about what we had done and what we planned to do. He was always interested in learning about our goals. Most of the time, Bettina and I dreaded these grillings. And my mom was no less driven: As one of the first female wireless operators at sea, she was a pioneer from an early age. She was also an electronics engineer, but she put this aside first when she married my dad, then later to raise the family in Montreal. When I was about fifteen, my brothers, Martin and Kris, moved to Norway for school, and my mom put Bettina and me through high school—private school, no less—while working as the only woman at a real estate investment firm. At the time, we didn't really understand what she had given up or what challenges she would face while raising us and forging a life as a woman in the male-dominated world of business. As for the decision to send us to private school: Trafalgar School for Girls in Montreal would play a large role in my life well beyond my formative years and into my adult life—and to this very day.

Though I dreaded my father's grillings, I was driven too. My first dream was to go to the moon, and after I mentioned this to my third-grade teacher, she encouraged me to write to NASA to secure my spot. So, I wrote a letter and was surprised to get a nice letter back encouraging me to stay in school, to keep learning math and science, and maybe one day they would let civilians into space. One day . . .

My second dream was to play tennis at Wimbledon. I chased that dream as far as attending the Harry Hopman Tennis Academy near Tampa, Florida. After moving to Newport Beach, California, I played tennis at the John Wayne Tennis Club (now called the Palisades Tennis Club), hired a professional coach, and got a job stringing racquets at Paramount Tennis on 17th Street in Costa Mesa, owned by two tennis fanatic brothers from New Jersey.

Tennis bred routine, stamina, focus, determination, and purpose—it demanded physical strength and agility. I loved and lived for tennis. It was the very thing that encouraged me to leave Canada at the age of nineteen and find myself. It gave me the confidence I needed to stand up for myself, both on and off the court.

I moved back to Canada a few years later to finish college, but I eventually made my way back to the US and found myself on Catalina Island, California, where Bettina also settled. My sister and I are best friends, and I adore her son—my nephew, Kjell—too. I feel such kinship with him and his spirit that I always say if I didn't know any better, I'd think he was my son. He's smart, kind, gentle, talented, athletic, and playful—just like his mom.

If you wanted to trace my whereabouts in my twenties, you'd have to put pushpins all over a map of the world. I spent a summer in Norway, attending summer school and studying Norwegian society, politics, and language. I worked at the first-ever twenty-four-hour gas station in Oslo, then moved to Catalina Island, where I was a waitress at Descanso Beach and worked at the Runway Café at the Catalina Airport and the Sandtrap Restaurant and Bar. I managed a vintage clothing store in Laguna Beach, California, ran a boutique, taught outdoors classes to youth and adults, and worked as a rock climbing and backpacking guide for at-risk kids from San Diego to Los Angeles. I did many things, in many places, and uprooted myself and my partners numerous times. Too numerous to count.

Even so, the truth is, I hate leaving people—that has always been the hardest part of following my dreams and taking risks. But this, too, is a skill I started learning as a child. After we immigrated to Canada, we moved. A lot. I became skilled at finding new friends and was, inevitably, accustomed to saying goodbye to them when we moved on. At ten or eleven years old, you don't spend a lot of time thinking about the impacts of moving and making new friends, but you certainly do when you get older, and looking back, I see that this constant moving was building the foundation for my future.

Add all this together, and you have a clear picture of my path toward the biggest change I ever made: uprooting everything I had built and going to Bamsebu for nine months. I knew it would be hard, but after all my experiences, I also knew I could do it. Even though nothing I had done up to that point had been as hard as what I was about to experience at Bamsebu, I felt confident that I was ready.

It helped that my work life had been weaving in and out of the Antarctic since the early nineties. At the age of thirty, I became part of the first American Women's Expedition (AWE) to ski across Antarctica, joining the team of Anne Dal Vera, Sue Giller, and Ann Bancroft. They had been planning and preparing for this expedition for five years when a team member dropped out after a training trip across Greenland. I showed up and was able to fill the void.

Synchronicity: a meaningful coincidence. I was in the right place at the right time. My partner at the time was Deborah Liv, an editor at *Footprints*, a publication by the outdoor retailer I worked for, Adventure 16. Deborah told me about AWE and mentioned that they were looking for a fourth team member, and it was her conviction about my inner strength and drive that gave me the courage to connect with the Expedition leader, Ann Bancroft. The power of words. Never, ever doubt how much power your words of encouragement can have on another.

Of course, venturing off always means leaving special people behind—the ones who incessantly show up with support and love. I've been beyond lucky to have many such people in my life, including Bettina, who has been there through thick and thin and who was right behind me on this newest adventure.

There are certain things in life you never forget. Things like those moments and adventures that strip you of all you have known, the hardships that shatter your ego and force you to redefine yourself without it, and the kind of pain that makes you rethink the meaning of strength and weakness, showing you with absolute clarity that asking for help is a sign of strength. Strength doesn't mean reaching the summit of your dreams alone—it means getting there as part of a community, sharing the load and showing your vulnerability. Your humanness.

For my team members of AWE and me, that load was about 90 kg (200 lbs)—the weight we each dragged behind us for sixty-seven days and 1,125 km (700 miles) from the edge of the Ronne Ice Shelf to the South Pole. The whole expedition was a moment of reckoning for me—I was the youngest and thought to be the strongest when I started out on this life-altering expedition. Slowly, those layers of strength were peeled back by successive illnesses and pain: bronchitis, tendonitis, swollen eyes, oedema, blistered feet, and cracked fingers. I became so weak that I had to give up part of my load, which was, in effect, the only thing I could control. Ah yes, the lesson of surrender—one we must experience time and time again. There are lessons you only learn once you're able to let go of your ego and any attachment to a certain outcome. Those lessons serve you well.

Given all this relinquishing of ego, perhaps it was no coincidence that giving a career-day presentation at Trafalgar back in 2010 left me questioning the mark I had left on the world and evaluating all of the hard lessons I have learned to date.

Since the South Pole, my legs have taken me up Kilimanjaro five times, a few times across Catalina Island for the annual Run Catalina marathon, across King George Island off Antarctica, over the Greenland ice sheet, along the Sierra High Route in the Sierra Nevada, and, best of all, along the length of the John Muir Trail with one of my favorite humans on the planet, my nephew Kjell. That was a trip I hold near and dear: Time in hiking boots with someone you love and a backpack on your back can bring enough joy and memories to sustain you through dark polar nights. Of which there were about to be many.

I first visited Svalbard in 2013 with an Arctic operator from Canada. As with every expedition voyage I've ever been on, the expedition team was off-the-charts spirited and full of life and passion for all things polar.

The Arctic is so unlike the Antarctic.

In the south, you have an actual landmass called Antarctica—the highest, driest, coldest, windiest, and brightest of the seven continents. It's roughly the size of the United States and Mexico combined and almost completely covered by a layer of ice that's more than 2–3 km (1¼–2 miles) thick on average, and nearly 5 km (3 miles) thick in places. The ice sheet holds more than 90 percent of the world's freshwater. Imagine that! Ninety percent of all the freshwater in the world is locked up in the continent of Antarctica. The South Pole—the point at 90 degrees latitude south—sits almost smack-dab in the middle of this landmass.

The Arctic north is very different in that there is no landmass around the North Pole.

Until two years ago, ice surrounded the North Pole throughout the year—but as we have all been witnessing, the ice in the Arctic Ocean has been diminishing rapidly. This is a dire problem for the entire Arctic ecozystem and for the biodiversity of species that depend on this ice—as well as for the world, since Arctic sea ice influences the climate and weather globally. Its bright whiteness reflects solar heat back into the atmosphere and insulates the ocean below, and the temperature differences between the cold Arctic and the hot tropics drive winds and ocean currents.

It's no coincidence that the expedition-cruise industry brought Hilde's path and mine together on that September day in 2016. We were both shaped by the natural world; we're both explorers and adventurers; both vibrant, healthy, and yearning to make an impact on the world; and we were both ready for another life-altering adventure. We each realized how fortunate we had been to grow up immersed in nature, and we wanted to protect that world so others could grow up enjoying it as we had. When we met, we surveyed the pushpins we had collectively marked all over the map, as well as our experiences with the friends, colleagues, employers, scientists, artists, changemakers, female leaders, visionaries, CEOs, and researchers we met along the way—and we wove all of these threads together to shape the foundation for *Hearts in the Ice*.

We would pay close attention to the heartbeats in the ice and use them to fuel our mission: to spread the word that the world needs saving, now more than ever before. And that it can be saved one project, one idea, and one person at a time.

HILDE

On Svalbard, I live more intimately with nature than ever before. In the twenty-five years I've lived up here, I have been fortunate to develop skills, whether on my many boat trips, snowmobile trips, expeditions, trekking and hunting trips with my husband Steinar, or hiking and skiing alone or with friends. I went on many ski expeditions lasting anywhere from one to three weeks, as both team member, guide, and expedition leader. Through my work and in my personal life I have seen most of Svalbard. The Arctic is a world of extremes, and if you're going to explore it, adaptation to the elements is a must.

I have always felt such a powerful attachment to all the Arctic had to offer: the changes from season to season, hues of light like I had never before seen, and the incessant harsh weather. I was so at home in this landscape—there was a kind of grounding here on Svalbard that I could actually feel physically. It made me feel like part of something much bigger than myself. In these challenging, magical surroundings, I felt small, but nonetheless strong.

I read literature about pioneers like Wanny Woldstad and Helfrid Nøis, two women who paved the way for the rest of us and harbored the dream of spending an entire winter in the wilderness and total isolation.

Then in 2010, I had the opportunity to take care of a trapper's station called Austfjordneset. The trapper, Tommy Sandal, had to leave for a few months and needed someone to take care of his five dogs and the station itself. I had a full-time job at the time, but I couldn't resist the opportunity, so I took a short leave from work and spent two months at that hunting station in Austfjorden, about 150 km (93 miles) north of Longyearbyen, with my friend Merete Flø.

That was where I began to love the simple life beyond the settlement of Longyearbyen. For a start, I quickly got a lot more experience in handling very close encounters with polar bears. Like the trapper Tommy did, Merete and I hunted seals to feed the dogs, and the seal slaughter was, of course, irresistible to the polar bears. We had more than a hundred visits from polar bears (127 to be specific) to the hunting station during our stay.

At this point, I had fifteen years of experience with polar bears under my belt, but with several dangerous encounters, I got to test my knowledge and perseverance even more.

Then, in 2013–14, I had a six-month assignment as a meteorology associate for the Norwegian Meteorological Institute at Bjørnøya, or "Bear Island," a small island between the mainland of Norway and Svalbard. This would push my limits again—for one thing, I had to quit my job! (But I got it back a year later.) And since Bjørnøya is very remote, the journey involved a thirty-hour boat trip from Longyearbyen. Next, I completed a shorter stay—two months—at another remote island, Jan Mayen, also as a meteorology associate.

These experiences—and the accompanying exposure to extreme Arctic weather, nature, and wildlife—often meant leaving my comfort zone. Without consciously realizing it, through all these experiences, I had been preparing for the challenge of spending a full winter in the Arctic, testing myself against the powers of nature and the loneliness that came with long winters.

They say that Norwegians are born with skis on their feet and, well, it's kind of true: I had skis on almost before I could walk. I grew up in Fjellhamar, a suburb of Oslo, as the youngest of four siblings: Nina, Arild, and Vidar, then me, born almost five years later. I had a safe and loving childhood, and my parents would take us out into the natural world often, with me in either a *pulka* sled or a backpack when they were out on ski trips.

When I first made it onto skis, it was just for short trips, then the trips got longer and longer. I remember always being tired! Growing up with older siblings has its advantages, and although I was considered the small, weak one in my younger years, they taught me to be resilient and strong and to stand up for myself.

Like every child, I developed a yearning to explore far beyond the mountains. With red rubber boots on my tiny feet, I embarked on journeys of discovery in our garden and in the little forest knoll behind our house in Fjellhamar. We called it Olser´n—a small but very exciting little hilltop with trees and bushes and an expansive ecozystem of insects, birds, squirrels, mice, and minks. It was my personal little eco-universe and a place I loved to explore and play. In the winter, we sledded and made snow caves and ski jumps, and in the summer, we climbed trees and built shelters out of fir branches.

Without realizing it, my first introduction to nature conservation came in the third grade. The municipality of Lørenskog wanted to build housing in my backyard and playground, my universe. Fear and then anger bubbled up amongst my classmates, my neighborhood, and myself. We were determined to fight for our space and make our voices heard. We got help making a little Styrofoam model of the area and wrote a deeply heartfelt letter to the county with a request that they not turn our paradise into a housing development. We traipsed up to the mayor's office with our written arguments and signatures.

And it worked! The area was partially designated as a recreational area; the county took some of it, but we got to keep most of it! It was the place that had given us scrapes, bruises, splinters, and wasp stings; that had taught us the sounds of woodpeckers and hooting owls; that had given us the scent of wet earth and sweet lilies. We were immensely proud and felt that our little world had been saved.

My family—including my dear grandfather, my only grandparent—gave me a solid upbringing and introduction to life and the natural world. My parents repaired and fixed things that fell apart; we had to as we couldn't afford to purchase new things when things broke. Even if I hated the fact that my wardrobe consisted of a lot of mended hand-me-downs from my siblings, that was my reality. We spent many holidays in the hut we built close to where my dad grew up—at the farm in Fredrikstad, where my dear Aunt Anne and Uncle Svein lived with their three children. Through both farming and hunting, I learned where food came from. We grew all sorts of things in our garden at Fjellhamar—berries, fruits and vegetables. And every autumn, we took trips to the forests nearby to pick mushrooms and wild berries. It wasn't until I moved to Svalbard in my late twenties that I officially became a big game hunter, but before then, I joined my dad on numerous hunting trips and amassed a lot of experience.

When I was twelve, I got my own dog, Nanok, a Siberian Husky. I began to dogsled in Nordmarka, outside Oslo, and was fascinated by the peace and quiet I experienced alone in nature with a team of dogs. My dream was to bring two or three dogs to our overwintering at Bamsebu, but I am so glad we decided on Ettra. A perfect choice.

Team sports like soccer and handball were a big part of my teenage years, too, along with two special lifelong friends, Elin Børrud and Elin Wethal. Nevertheless, skiing had been part of my upbringing, I started downhill skiing late in my teens with my first boyfriend, Johny. Downhill and off-piste skiing have been some of my favorite activities ever since—so much so that I co-founded Svalbard Ski & Sail (now Svalbard Expeditions) in 2018. I also love the long, slow life of cross-country skiing, especially with a heavy pulka behind me, loaded with all I need for the next few weeks.

For years I invited Steinar to join me for an overwintering. He was not thrilled by the thought of a small trapper's hut surrounded by darkness and polar bears for months. Still, Steinar become the single most important person to make this overwintering at Bamsebu possible.

I feel so privileged to have had such a rich and fulfilllling life and exciting work. Through my twenty-five years in Spitsbergen Travel/Hurtigruten Svalbard, I have had the opportunity to see and experience a lot of the Arctic and the Antarctic. I have been part of the development of the tourist industry at Svalbard. I have been part of the journey that has taken more than we have given. I'm lucky enough to have many friends who are important to me: my two Elins, Anne-Lise, Lea, Bente, Merete, Anne-Margrethe, and all the people I've built strong, deep relationships with throughout my childhood, my work, and my life on Svalbard. My colleagues have come from all over the world, and we've worked together on land and at sea or on small islands, way out in the Arctic seas. Through my work and my personal experiences, I have developed an amazing network. It has all added up to an exciting journey, complete with challenges that have shaped me and defined my identity.

And I have always been curious. Ever since I faced the challenges of too-long ski trips or too-high treetops to climb as a child, I have sought out new challenges and unfamiliar terrain. In this, I've had great support from my parents, my siblings, and my own family: Steinar, Frode, and Susanne. This support served as the foundation upon which to live my dream: an overwintering at Bamsebu, and by a remarkable and aligned extension, our joint project, *Hearts in the Ice*. A dream together with Sunniva that started as an idea and became a reality. An opportunity to live a life immersed in nature, experiencing the changes in the seasons and the wildlife and doing what felt natural—to communicate and share knowledge together with experts and collect data for scientists—and with new knowledge, to protect what we both love: our natural world.

CHAPTER 3

SELF-ISOLATION

Sometimes the Heart Must Lead the Way

*Mental health is based on a certain degree of tension, the tension
between what one has already achieved and what one still ought to
accomplish, or the gap between what one is and what one should become
. . . . What man actually needs is not a tensionless state but rather the
striving and struggling for a worthwhile goal, a freely chosen task.*
— Viktor Frankl

When we left the "civilized world" for Bamsebu in September 2019, not many people truly understood what self-isolation really meant. Who would ever have imagined that within a year, the entire world would be familiar with the term and would have a personal experience built around it? For us, the term would mean complete self-sufficiency, remote from any help, and far away from the people we love. Far away, in fact, from *any* people. Sheltered from any and all of the usual distractions: traffic, streetlights, signs, the hum of cars on the road, free Wi-Fi or data, stores, even somewhere to go if we were missing something, like a spare part. At Bamsebu, we were completely alone and isolated.

This life might sound simple, and on the one hand, it is—but to live so far from anything (and anyone) requires a tremendous amount of preparation, patience with yourself, daily vigilance, hard work, and keen problem-solving abilities. We aren't electricians or plumbers or contractors. We couldn't pick up the phone and call in a technician to come between the hours of noon and two p.m. to assess then fix our problem. Instead, we had to solve every problem through one careful, patient thought and action at a time.

Our guts, intuition, logic—our hearts—have led the way.

A hurricane hammered the walls of our little cabin, Bamsebu. Each ear-splitting noise came with a force so great it could easily have ravaged our home. We were rattled. Mounds of snow had piled up along the outside walls, which at least made the cabin feel better anchored and a little less vulnerable. It was nearly impossible to open the outer door, which was probably for the best. There wasn't much to see anyway: It was completely dark and too dangerous to go outside under these conditions. The door opens outward, and with gusts of wind blowing at sixty miles per hour, it might have been ripped right off its hinges. We couldn't hear anything but the wind pounding against everything in its path—until we heard a rumbling sound . . . the door to our food-storage shed banging around in the storm.

It was critical that we found a way to close that door so the polar bears wouldn't help themselves to our limited supply of food. So, despite our trepidation, we managed to get that outer door open and carefully made our way outside. Dealing with a door that's being tossed around by such strong winds was an almost impossible task and a dangerous undertaking. The right gust of wind could have ripped it off and struck us down dead or splintered it into a million pieces. We soon saw that the hinges had been torn right out of the door's base! We were amazed at the power of nature, a force beyond taming.

Together, we were able to steady the door and coax it back to its original position. This time, the wind was an ally, helping us push the door into place. It didn't help with our communication, though: Every time we tried to talk to each other, we had to yell so loud that it hurt, hurling our words into the path of the wind. It's times like this that patience factors large, and you learn how to communicate with your eyes, hand gestures, and nods of the head. We reattached the hinges with our Dewalt drill and got the door secured well enough that it would take more than a storm to dislodge it again. What a relief—our food was safe from the polar bears, for now. But we wouldn't have access to it as long as this storm continued—it was just too risky to be outside. Luckily, there was enough food inside the cabin to last us a few days. It took two more days for the weather to settle down enough for us to hang the door properly, with functioning hinges. That job required careful cooperation and some physical effort, but we made it happen—and what a victory! We felt such a sense of accomplishment looking at the door, back in its place and more secure than before the storm took it.

The door wasn't the only casualty of those hurricane winds. We noticed that we had been disconnected from the world too: no Wi-Fi. Our network was down. This was not good. It's hard to describe the feeling of having no way of communicating with the outside world. It's sort of a desperate feeling since to be at Bamsebu without connectivity is to be completely isolated and vulnerable. It was just not safe. We went outside to inspect. The wind had slammed down the lid of the grey Pelican case that held the MCD-MissionLINK, and the antenna had been broken clean off. No antenna, no satellite, no service. The antenna contained wire cord that kept us connected to the world out there, and when the antenna broke, the wire inside was severed.

The wire itself is so small that repairing it seemed like an impossible task. But we hadn't given up on any task so far, and this would not be the first. After a lot of fumbling around, both of us, and several dozen attempts and hours fiddling, we were able to carefully weave replacement wires inside the cable. We waited . . . then there it was, the green blinking light! Finally, a connection! *Yessssss!!!* We were so proud; it was such a great feeling. By now, we really felt that we could hire ourselves out as electricians and general repairwomen. Whatever it is, we can do it! That night Sunniva made a special dinner to celebrate!

The version of self-isolation that spread through society with Covid-19 isn't quite the same as our isolation at Bamsebu, but there are some similar requirements and necessary adaptations. On a national level, every country has had to engage in some form of self-sufficiency. From what we learned, governments were forced to get creative and build temporary clinics in order to offer citizens access to medical care. Top scientists, data analyzts, and medical professionals were recruited for their care and expertise. Organizations quickly mobilized to enable their employees to work from home, and even restaurants adapted, building out specialized menus and access to food that could be taken away and cooked at home. Many people around the world began to trust their intuition, listen to science, and rely on their guts, which told them to stay home and keep themselves and their loved ones safe. Some people may have used the time to better themselves financially, while others may have taken the opportunity to reflect on their day-to-day lives and make changes to give themselves the best life moving forward. All this time in isolation seems to have forced people to truly listen to their hearts and see the inequities in the world.

The lessons we learned during our stay at Bamsebu—sitting alone, without interruption or anywhere far to go—are essentially the same lessons society was forced to learn. We learned how creative and flexible we can be when we have to rely on exactly what we have. We became MacGyvers, both handy women, able to fix anything as long as we took the time and patience to figure it out. We didn't sweat the small stuff. We dropped things, broke things, spilled things, but it was always okay and not worth wasting energy on. We gave each other space when needed. We were living in tight quarters, so we learned to respect our differences. Our different skillsets were part of our success, and we learned how to play off that and worked together really well. We learned, too, how valuable it is to tell people that they matter, write them, call them. Even though we were so far away, we felt closer to the people we cared about since we would hold space for them, talk about them over dinner, and think about them even though we couldn't be with them in person. If only they knew how much they all mattered.

And we came to understand how little we really need to survive, how resilient we are. We didn't shower for nine months, since there was no running water. We conserved what fresh water we had, and we recycled water so we could do dishes and wash clothes. We learned not to trust the "best by" dates stamped on eggs and food packages. If you take care of these items, they last. We rotated the eggs and kept our root vegetables cool and under the bed, where it was dark. We didn't waste any food because we couldn't shop. What we brought at the start of our expedition was what we had. We learned to reuse our clothes, and that wool lasts a lot longer than any synthetic fabric. We developed a new understanding of the inequities of a world in which so many people don't have access to food, water, shelter, and clothing, while a small percentage of us waste these things. We came to appreciate the gift of staying in one place and not traveling, and to experience the beauty right outside our door and in our backyard.

And if we had to give you one learning, one piece of advice, from that time, it would be this: Be willing to put in the time to define what you value and how you live. Ask yourself: What does "living" mean, and how am I living? Am I a taker or a giver?

Nine Months at Bamsebu Become a Year

Our nine months at Bamsebu turned into a year as we watched and waited for the Covid-19 virus to finish its ravages and settle down. But of course, it never did settle down, and instead, we had to adjust our expectations.

So, what happens when you spend a year in a remote cabin in the Arctic? Our year was a journey filled with adaptation, danger, challenges, joy, and sorrow. A journey through the enormously varied seasons, through the polar night—and all in an area where only a few life forms are able to survive. This fairy tale of ours is full of encounters with nature so profound that they're almost impossible to describe. We might never be able to fully describe them. Nevertheless, we wrote down some tidbits that might paint the best portrait of our life at Bamsebu:

- A year where we got to decide how strong we wanted to be, both physically and psychologically, and work toward that goal. We traded in going to the gym for yoga inside our tiny hut, fitness bands, runs on the tundra, and long walks with Ettra.
- A journey within ourselves in a vast, unexplored landscape that provides extreme joy, endless wonder, unfamiliar feelings, and demands patience and effort. We traded in extensive travel for donning snowmobile suits, dry suits, and cold-weather gear to enjoy our own backyard.
- A time in our lives without any external noise in the form of cell phones, computers, telephones, traffic, or pressure from looming deadlines or ringing doorbells. We traded the news for listening to our inner voices.

- A year of deciding how to live based on the fundamental things we needed in order to survive. We traded in hot showers, running water, electricity, and shopping to live with solar and wind power and worked hard to leave a zero footprint, using only what we brought.
- A time in our lives when we were truly immersed in everything around us. The forces of nature. Wildlife. Sounds. Silence. Peace. Calm. The storm. Polar night. Midnight sun. Complete, perfect stillness inside.
- A time in our lives when we chose to self-isolate, with no idea what impact it would have on us and our lives until it was over. We went from feeling like we knew a lot to understanding just how little we knew. We came to understand and appreciate what it really means to hold up a mirror to yourself.
- A remote stay that would change radically when the world out there was hit hard and turned upside down by a global pandemic. There we were, so far from the daily news, any threat of infection, and the reality of the devastation facing villages, countries, and people everywhere. For us, there was no threat of a virus of any kind. Through this pandemic, we came to understand how inter-twined all of our lives are and how we might have something to teach others about coping, surviving, and thriving.
- A time in our lives when we anchored the power of collaboration as evidenced by experts willing to share their data and observa-tions with youth around the world in our twice-monthly school calls.
- Bearing witness to the circle of life—following the four seasons in the Arctic and how the entire Arctic comes to life after months of darkness.
- Simple living and simple joys. A hammock, a sauna, a polar swim, singing, dancing, a spa day, skiing, running, golf, flying a drone, an outdoor grill, kayaking, movie night, and celebrating everything possible—even the last carrot, candlelight, small presents, and effort and putting care into every meal. Celebrating birthdays, our own and others.
- A life where repair, reuse, and recycle becomes a daily and nec-essary habit.

- A life where our loved ones felt closer, though they had never been further away, because we had time to think about them in ways so profound.
- A time in life where gratitude has never been more present.
- Living the dream.

It was that final point that would leave the biggest impression on us. We felt helpless in many ways, observing from afar as everything we knew seemed to collapse so easily. Then there was the fear—fear that something might happen to our loved ones while we were so far away and couldn't do anything about it. Like everyone else, we would find ourselves needing to adapt, exercise our resilience, be creative, question our values, and revise our plans. Plan B, here we come!

LIFE IN AND AROUND BAMSEBU

The trapper's cabin, Bamsebu, is referred to as a "kulturminne"—a cultural heritage building—a title automatically given to all structures built in Svalbard before 1945. When a building has this designation, it means that no one can alter anything on the outside—it must stay authentic. So even those rusty hinges on the windows must be handled carefully—even in -35°C (-31°F) temperatures with hurricane winds. To say the cabin is vulnerable to the elements is an understatement.

The cabin is uninsulated, made from old wood slats, and reinforced with round log posts, added to protect the hut from polar bear break-ins. There are four little windows: two facing east, one to the north, and one facing west. It was built around 1930 by Ingvald Svendsen (prebuilt elements like parts for walls and roof were brought from the mainland of Norway) as a station for hunting beluga whales and used by whale hunters throughout the summer. The whale hunters had large wooden boats they'd use to row out heavy-duty fishing nets. Then, when the white beluga whales came into the bay to feed on bait, they would lock them in by rowing out with the nets and securing them behind them. They would then shoot the white whales in the head with a rifle and drag them up onto the beach. A relatively humane hunt, as hunts go. They would use the blubber for oil and the skin for machinery belts and ski bindings since it's so full of oil that it never dries out and remains pliable and strong for years.

The area around Bamsebu—a popular spot for visits from the expedition cruise industry—is full of reminders of those beluga-hunting days. To be here is to live with the remains and reminders of the decimation of a species. On the beach below the cabin lie the skeletons and skulls of thousands of beluga whales—proof of the first major industry on Svalbard. There are eleven large piles of bones along the shoreline. Bamsebu is in a fjord—an inlet with steep sides, usually created by a glacier—called Van Keulenfjorden, and the adjoining bays, Ingebrigtsbukta and Kapp Fleur de Lys, were the most popular spots for beluga hunting. The most favorable hunting conditions were found here at the mouth of the fjord. A little further to the southwest, in Rechecherfjorden, there are two more areas where beluga were hunted: Jernbekken and Lægerneset. The first successful overwinter stay in the region was completed at Lægerneset in 1630–31, when eight Englishmen were stranded after heavy ice conditions made it impossible to pick them up at the end of the hunting season. Remarkably, seven of the eight survived this unplanned winter stay, according to cultural heritage advisor and author Per Kyrre Reymert.

Down at Kapp Fleur de Lys, on a beach called Kvitfiskstrand (White Fish Beach), a few kms northwest of Ingebrigtsbukta, lie a few well-preserved wooden boats that were used for beluga hunting. Meanwhile, Bamsebu is surrounded by the scant remains of three wooden boats and a little shack called Skarpsyn, meaning "clear lookout," which lies about 60 meters (200 feet) south of Bamsebu, with one of the three wooden boats turned upside down next to it. In fact, this upturned boat was used for lodging during the summer hunt. There's a small foundation that supports the gunwale of the boat, creating nearly enough height for a person to stand up straight underneath it. Measurements and drawings of that unique "cabin" were made in 1936 by geologist Anders Orvin, and the name given to it was Hotæl Blanke Kniven, which translates to "Hotel Shiny Knife." Maybe it got its name from the steel that served as protection under the keel of the boat. The sketch included a bunk bed, a small table, a stool, and a little stove. There was just enough space for one man, and it was probably in high demand since the main Bamsebu cabin was likely very crowded.

In the 1980s, Bamsebu was restored by three miners: Jack, Knut, and Otto. When they started their "rescue work" on the cabin, it was in a state of total disrepair. Windows and doors were gone, and the whole cabin was filled with a large block of ice with enormous fishing nets frozen into it—all still there from a hunt that ended almost fifty years earlier. Over the course of two winters, going by snowmobiles on frozen fjords and across the glaciers and mountain ranges from Svea to Bamsebu, they got the cabin fixed up and then began to camp there together. The cabin is their private property, but none of them lives on Svalbard anymore, so many years ago, they arranged to transfer the responsibility of the cabin to a friend—Hilde's husband, Steinar Strøm. Hilde and Steinar have been traveling to Bamsebu since 1996 for long weekends and Easter vacations.

Among the repairs the three miners made to the cabin was to add a small shed with an outhouse. However, after several close encounters with polar bears while using the original outhouse, which stood 20 meters (66 feet) from the main cabin, the three men moved the outhouse so that it was attached to the main hut. This didn't stop the polar bears, though—the cabin was vandalized by intruding bears each year until 2000 when the men secured it with logs angled against the walls and up to the roof. These logs help to protect the cabin from break-ins, as they disturb the polar bear's space to maneuver. In fact, there hasn't been a polar bear inside Bamsebu since they were put up.

These were not the only precautions taken to protect the cabin from polar bears. The four wooden window shutters have large protruding nails on the outside, making the windows less appealing to bears as a point of entry. And in front of the door to the outside—which is relatively flimsy and has a little window—there is a large steel door that is locked when the cabin is unoccupied to give yet another layer of protection. During our stay at Bamsebu, we pulled the steel door as close as possible to the front door when we went to bed for extra security while we slept. But the truth is, if a polar bear wants in, it'll get in. They are enormously powerful, and their will to explore is very strong. They certainly won't politely knock on the windows or doors, waiting to be let in. They could burst through the walls or roof if they wanted to. But from inside the cabin, our senses were finely tuned to even the slightest of noise, so we would hear them and have time to scare them away.

Carefully scattered outside were our supplies, which had to last for close to a year. If they weren't outside around the hut, they were inside on shelves, under the couch, under our beds, or up in the small shed, Skarpsyn. Deciding what to bring on the trip involved multiple Excel spreadsheets, hundreds of phone calls, thousands of emails, and hours of time difference between the two of us in Canada and Norway. Daunting, to say the least, since if we ran out of anything, forgot to anticipate any potential emergencies or breakages, or ended up lacking a part or tool, we would be in deep trouble. Those were the moments we had to unpack our bags of patience. Our patience was eternally tested at Bamsebu, and the only choice was to just plain *figure it out*. We would often call on our problem-solving skills—and not just to deal with emergencies or breakages, but for every aspect of daily life. We were far from life's everyday comforts—in fact, we didn't shower for close to nine months. If that doesn't test a friendship, what will?

We took many boxes and crates of random tools and supplies, but truth be told, it was always hard to keep a real grasp on exactly what we had and where. If we ever thought we needed a special tool or part to fix something and we couldn't find it, we learned to visualize what else might work. *Clearly*, we would say, *there is something around here that will work.* This brought out our creativity and ended up being a skill we both honed.

The exterior of Bamsebu is all about logistics and practical needs. On the east-facing side, there were four large wooden boxes containing firewood that we chopped ourselves throughout the year. In the summer, we cut up the Siberian driftwood we collected on our boat, and in the winter, we dragged logs from a distant shore back to the hut with our snowmobiles. On the same side, there's a large stump that's been there for decades, sitting next to a wooden sawhorse, which we used to cut logs. It was as rickety as the hinges on the shutters, but it did the job.

On the west-facing side was an 800-litre (211-gallon) intermediate bulk container (IBC), which contained all of our fresh water. It was easy to get obsessed with the fear of running out of water and firewood, the two items that determined our well-being at the cabin. There's no insulation at Bamsebu, so without firewood, we'd have had no way to heat the inside as the cold air screamed through the antiquated floorboards. Neither would we have been able to cook—though we had a small two-burner propane stove that saved us on occasion, our primary cooking element was our wood-burning stove. Then there was the second fear: *What if we run out of water?* Did we dare even think about that?

The fear of running out of anything certainly crossed our minds. We knew the water source was poor in the area, but there was another thought that overpowered even that: It was impossible not to think about how much we had overused in our lives up until then. Now that we were forced to ration everything inside the hut, from water to firewood to food to clothing, this thought resurfaced over and over again. In our lives outside of Bamsebu, access to most things felt unlimited. Normally, we wouldn't think twice before tossing food from the pantry or replacing something that wasn't that old, just because it was cracked or chipped. The list of things that are easily tossed is long.

Outside, we stored several aluminum ZARGES cases filled with supplies for our citizen-science projects as well as all sorts of gadgets: containers of filtered salt water, a saw, an ice ladle and filter, plastic bottles, a special tent for our insect capturing (mainly different types of small flies surviving the cold weather), alcohol for our samples, an ice-core cutting board, shovels, polar bear poop bags and sample bottles, a measuring stick, a CastAway CTD device for gauging the temperature and depth of sea water, a Secchi disk, a phytoplankton net, extra water bottles, a filtering device and filters for the phytoplankton, Lugol samples, boxes of sanitary gloves, tweezers, and squeeze bottles. We had the longest drill bit either of us had ever seen: It was bright red, 1.15 meters (3 feet, 8 inches) long and 9 cm (4 inches) in diameter, and it sat inside its own long, rectangular case. We used it for our ice-core drilling—and might we add, it was a hand drill!

We got electricity for lights and to charge devices through a solar cell, when there was light outside, and by way of a windmill that harnessed the nearly constant wind. A man named Dag at Power Controls set up batteries and a power station for us in the entryway, and it was these that we charged with our solar and wind power. We also had a so-called fuel cell, which burned methanol to charge the batteries during periods of low wind and no light during the Arctic winter, when we needed electricity to light the indoors to charge the computer and Iridium telephone, to power a small freezer and floodlights, and for our headlamps, chainsaw batteries, and the MCD-MissionLINK, our satellite transmitter. Methanol is easy on the environment, releasing only water vapor when burned. It was good to have that kind of backup at times, and it felt fantastic to use green energy and harness the potent forces outside our walls to provide power inside.

We had everything we needed either inside Bamsebu or up in the wooden shed, Skarpsyn. Since Skarpsyn was built around 1930, whatever went in it needed to be waterproof. It was made from driftwood that's now grey and very worn, and there isn't a single level wall, which means the floorboards are also crooked. The wooden door has to be carefully opened since it sits on rusty hinges. And it was inside this damp, rickety shed that our life was tucked away in bags we had both amassed over the years from The North Face, Gregory, A16, Eagle Creek, and Outdoor Research, all of which had weathered the test of time. However, it's one thing to stuff things away into a bag and another to remember exactly what's in each bag, so in our haste, we tried to label the bags before they got stacked on top of each other. Since our storage space is limited here, we have become master space savers. Sunniva was the one who usually had full control of where to find the last bag of Cheetos or a can of peaches.

In spite of our rather scant space, we turned Bamsebu into a cozy, warm home—quite different from the cabin where beluga hunters lived among spears, hunting nets, and bone remnants. Not a day went by that we didn't light a candle to give the interior a soft glow, and during the darkest part of the year, we hung strings of lights to brighten things. We did whatever we could to create a homey atmosphere. Every evening, we made it a point to set the table, complete with folded napkins and colored wooden tulips for each of us. We would then sit down, light a candle, and eat dinner together. We would use each napkin for several days until it was "used up," but even so, the ritual created something of a celebratory feeling. We also put effort into cooking our food and enjoyed every single bite.

There was no filter: We gave ourselves permission to express our feelings and be gentle and emotional. We also tried to find something to celebrate every day. It could be a task we completed, like taking an amazing photo or managing a safe and successful phytoplankton collection that was challenging during the cold, harsh winter. Or we would make a point to verbally appreciate something that stirred us—the northern lights, the sliver of the moon, or the midnight sun. It wasn't at all unusual for us to pick someone we knew who we wanted to appreciate a little extra and celebrate them over a dinner conversation. After all, life is only as exciting and fun as you make it.

Gratitude became a solid part of our everyday lives. Over time, we shifted into the mindset we needed—that no matter how dark or physically exhausting a day might be, we could always come back to a place of gratitude. We always reminded each other how lucky we were and thanked each other for the efforts we made with the cooking, firewood, ice or water, dishes, and everything else that made our partnership successful. We each kept our own little gratitude notebook to write down what we were grateful for each day. It served as a daily reminder that there's always something to be grateful for!

Neither one of us was an expert in coping with isolation or thriving together, so we often sought outside help. Before we left, Carina Vinberg from Framgångare and Kit Jackson from Strategy Together gave us notebooks, among other tools, that they felt would support us. Their advice included exercises such as identifying your own values, working through goal-setting exercises, and establishing strategies to better focus on the present. We'll admit that this didn't always come easily and there were times it felt a little tedious or time-consuming, but it was important work. It helped us to develop the right mental tools, build a solid foundation, solidify our values, and train our thought patterns such that we would be able to remain in good spirits and not be consumed by things like the darkness, the solitude, random comments, or misread body language. Doing the work to become mentally strong is just as important as physical training. We learned not just to survive but to *thrive.*

Aside from wearing heavy belts with flare guns and slinging rifles over our shoulders, it was also important for us to be women—to show our feminine sides. Hilde's long history of wearing lace underwear instead of training bras made it such that we both got several sets of gorgeous PrimaDonna undergarments given to us. Often, women hide or mask their femininity, believing it will make them seem less strong and professional. But why? As women, we should be proud to be exactly who we are, with unique insights, compassion, and intuition to offer in the sphere of leadership. While men are often expected to remain stoic, strong, and direct, women can be a breath of fresh air, balancing those staunch characteristics with empathy and collaboration.

Even while spending the winter at Bamsebu in icy-cold temperatures, we continued to embrace our feminine qualities. The tough exteriors likely portrayed in our photos were paired with femininity on the inside. We had coping tools, survival skills, weapons—and bright red heels! For Christmas and New Year's Eve, we went all-out, putting on our cocktail dresses, throwing on our heels, even washing our hair and putting on a little mascara for the first time in months, and letting our feminine sides loose! It was quite the scene: the biting wind cutting through the walls, snow piled up outside, and polar bears roaming around out there somewhere while we were in this tiny hut called Bamsebu, embracing our femininity. It was nearly 30 degrees below zero (-22°F), but our table was decorated with traditional Norwegian Christmas food. Joy! There were gifts, too, sent from near and far, and greetings shared in letters and virtual messages. These letters and gifts were sent well in advance of our departure from Longyearbyen, and we stashed them all up in Skarpsyn until it was time to pull the packages out and unpack the contents. It felt like everyone we knew had kept us in their thoughts that day. We had so many letters with "Date to Open" birthdays, holidays, and special occasions. It was such a beautiful slice into the lives of all of the people we cared so deeply about. Our friend Carina had made us an Advent calendar, which we opened with excitement every single day leading up to Christmas.

Here's a Christmas excerpt from Hilde's journal:

December 24.

Imagine waking up on Christmas Eve at Bamsebu! Minus 24 degrees outside [-11°F], and calm weather. Ettra came inside, and since Santa Claus had been here earlier in the month, we had our coffee and our Christmas stockings in Hilde's bed. We ate some of our Christmas goodies—coconut macaroons and gingerbread. We enjoyed a Christmas trivia game and learned a thing or two about Norwegian Christmas traditions! As I was talking to Lea on the phone, there came a knock at the door. Santa!? Santa was wearing long red underwear, a red jacket, and a long elf hat, and she had a big bag of gifts on her back and was called Sunniva!

We had to go up to Skarpsyn in dresses and thin stockings in -24°C [-11°F] weather, with deep snowbanks over the stream. We needed a new can of propane for a little extra cooking that night—the wood-burning stove was in full swing.

We thoroughly enjoyed a real Norwegian Christmas dinner of ribs, Christmas sausage, sauerkraut, gravy, cauliflower, broccoli, homemade mashed potatoes, and cranberry sauce. What a luxury! What a joy! The cabin was warm and decorated for Christmas; there were candles everywhere, and the red curtains and tablecloths created a memorable atmosphere. We opened letters and gifts and talked about, and with, our families all evening. Ettra enjoyed a bone and all the wrapping paper. It was a magical Christmas Eve at Bamsebu.

Polar Girls outside the front door of our home in Bamsebu.

Training run on the ice.

The team in Longyearbyen.

One of them is heading closer!

*One-and-a-half-year-old cub;
it was still with its sibling and their mum
but was very curious about us!*

Built for weather—Indrorobotics drone and Rolex.

Svalbard reindeer. The background, facing north is Malbukta.

Kayaking in May—we never leave without our safety gear! Bamsebu in the background.

March 2020—Pastel polar light.

Reindeer outside Bamsebu. The background, facing west, shows the mountains tops, Aclive kammen—Recherche fjord.

Capturing the "rare" cusp Aurora for Aurorasaurus.

Arctic Sunset in the west, toward Rechecher f ord.

Training is good for mental and physical health!

Magical February light at Kapp Fleur de Lys.

Hilde celebrating Norwegian National Day while in Bamsebu.

Drone pic of us with our ORU kayaks!

Norwegian Polar Institute monitors her (N26131) with a neck collar that measures movements and body temperature.

Celebrating the light!

Bearded seal on our kayak trip.

CHAPTER 4

HUNGRY CITIZEN SCIENTISTS

Curiosity

Hearts in the Ice is more than a project, more than two brave women managing to stay on their own during a polar winter. It is a model for how scientists, industrial partners, explorers, artists, and other stakeholders can meet in a common action to focus on polar climate changes. They are following in the footsteps of other polar pioneers, but this time not hunting for fur and skins, but knowledge and wisdom.
— Børge Damsgård

For most of the history of science, the very concept of citizen science would have been redundant. Most science was done by amateurs—by everyday people with a passionate interest in a topic, area, or idea. These amateurs had a deep curiosity that drove them to find answers.

Then science became formalized: Programs were developed and universities offered degrees in various areas of specialty. The need for citizen input lessened, and it grew harder to conduct public discussions around science and its social implications. But as we have seen with all great social movements, it's the power of the people, observations by many, and the voices of the collective that truly spark great change—not the voices of those in power.

We're in a very interesting moment, living through both the climate crisis, the nature crisis with the loss of species, and the Covid-19 crisis. Science and scientific research help us to understand trends and changes over time, and if we heed the science, it can lead us to make informed decisions. And yet there's a great divide between science, scientists, and the general public. Citizen science has the potential to bridge that divide. It challenges the norms of who is welcomed into the world of science.

At the age of fifty-six and dying of breast cancer, Rachel Carson, the American writer, scientist, and conservationist, stood up and testified before a US Senate subcommittee on the use of pesticides. She didn't tell anyone she was dying, and she worked hard to hide her frailty. She could barely walk, and she wore a wig. It was 1963; her book *Silent Spring* had come out about a year prior and started the largest environmental movement the world had seen. Her intention was to sound the alarm about the use of pesticides, the responsibility of science, and the limits of technological progress. She didn't expect to alter the course of history, but she did. Her writing initiated a transformation in the relationship between humans and the natural world and stirred an awakening of public environmental consciousness. She remains an example of what one committed individual can do to change the direction of society. Never doubt the power of one!

Hearts in the Ice draws inspiration from Rachel Carson as well as from Norwegian botanist Hanna Resvoll-Holmsen, the first female scientist on Svalbard and the first to advocate for protection of the environment both here on Svalbard and in mainland Norway. Hanna was fierce and dedicated and known to camp with two tents: one for herself and the other for her plants. A gifted writer and activist, she was skilled at engaging the press in her efforts to protect the natural world she studied and loved so dearly.

Then there's Dr Jane Goodall, an unparalleled figure in the world of science and conservation. Her work studying chimpanzees began in Africa in 1960 when neither of us was born. In the decades since, she has had a profound impact on how the world perceives animal intelligence, Earth's ecozystem, and the role of humanity within it.

Up until Carson, the American writer and philosopher Henry David Thoreau was the world's most celebrated environmentalist. In his book about living in the woods, *Walden*, he famously wrote, "I went to the woods because I wished to live deliberately, to front only the essential facts of life, and see if I could not learn what it had to teach, and not, when I came to die, discover that I had not lived." This statement has inspired us, and many others, to pare down and live simply. The quote itself raises the question, "What do we really need?"—a question we confronted when we found ourselves 140 kms (87 miles) from the nearest neighbor, surrounded by ice, in a fjord that rendered us entirely isolated for many months. Living intimately with nature, with the formidable responsibility and privilege to collect, record, observe, and document our surroundings for seven different research entities, we truly lived by Thoreau's great quote, along with a great deal of dedication, scientific information, and inspiration taken from those three remarkable women pioneers: Carson, Resvoll-Holmsen, and Goodall.

We each learned of the term "citizen science" and what it entails through our former employers, the polar operators Hurtigruten and Polar Latitudes. Our work with them was the first time we witnessed average, nonscientist citizens getting excited and curious about science as it relates to interpreting the natural world and its resources and studying impacts of climate change.

Next, we were introduced to research projects that are collecting data on land, underwater, and in the sky, and we connected with scientists and their projects. It became evident to us and to the scientists we spoke to that we would be able to contribute valuable data during our nine-month overwintering and enhance the collective understanding around the rapid changes in the Arctic. So, we decided to do just that. We started making phone calls, walking through the data protocol for each project, discussing how long each protocol might take on good and bad weather days, discussing how much equipment was needed, and so on. Initially, it was daunting to think of how much time this might take, and we wondered if we would be able to fulfillll our promises.

But if we could, it would be so worth it. After a few months of routine and repetitive experimentation, we felt comfortable with each project and how exactly to collect, record, and store the data and samples.

At its best, citizen science has the power to transform science and society. We live in a time when technology and information are abundant, and with access to both so widespread, it only makes sense to share information and collaborate on research that can help us all to better understand the impact our changing climate is having on our wildlife, microorganizms, ice, weather, and people. Citizen science has made it possible for people around the world to collect data and observations for thousands of projects that have real scientific value. Data collected by citizen scientists have shaped policy and initiated breakthroughs in research. Our planet and resources benefit from all of us being curious and engaged. In the future, we plan to advocate for more formal roles for citizen science ambassadors around the world.

While we are the nucleus of *Hearts in the Ice*, the project contains a community of heartbeats and a network of science partners and sponsors, each as unique as a snowflake, yet each aligned and connected in its own way to what we were trying to do at Bamsebu for science, innovation, education, and technology. There are likely dozens of science projects we could have been involved in, but we stuck to the ones that were most closely related to our understanding of human-induced climate change. We collected saltwater and phytoplankton samples and measured sea temperatures for Scripps Institution of Oceanography and the Fjord Phyto project, observed the phenomenal aurora and cloud types for NASA via its Globe Observer program and Aurorasaurus, flew timed flight plans using an InDro Robotics drone for the British Columbia Institute of Technology (BCIT) to capture color and thermal images of the landscape around Bamsebu and beyond, observed and recorded wildlife observations including polar bears for the Norwegian Polar Institute (NPI), and collected insect samples, kelp and the microscopic algae blooming in ice cores for the University Center in Svalbard (UNIS). We also collected snow samples and plastic debris and inspected the stomach linings of dead fulmars for the Norwegian Polar Institute (NPI).

Some people have asked: Why did we do this and what impact will it have?

We did it because we could and because we care. The data collected paints a story of change over time. We were in a place, the Arctic, where climate change is accelerated. If we could find a new species underwater, bring even a drop more understanding to the question of whether phytoplankton thrive in the polar night, or increase understanding of the patterns of polar bear visits and their possible responses to adaptation like hunting reindeer for food, we knew that everyone would benefit. After all, we know that what's happening in the Arctic doesn't stay here.

Here's what our UNIS protocol has to say about why sampling sea ice is so important:

Hearts in the Ice: The Importance of Sea Ice Sampling.

From February to May of 2020, the Hearts in the Ice project collected twelve sea-ice cores for the University Center in Svalbard (UNIS) to investigate the microscopic animals that live within the ice (sympagic meiofauna).

Although sea ice might look relatively lifeless from above, its interior can be teeming with microscopic life. A labyrinth of so-called "brine channels" (usually less than 1 mm [0.04 inches]) offers a refuge and feeding ground to various small animals from the seafloor and water column and for their offspring in the spring. They mainly feed on the high concentrations of nutritious microscopic algae that also live within the ice. At its peak bloom, up to 400,000 species per square meter [per 10.7 square feet] have been found in sea ice, but little is known about the identity of these small critters.

Since sea ice in the Arctic, and especially Svalbard, is diminishing much faster than anticipated, it is important to understand the ecological role it has in Arctic coastal ecozystems.

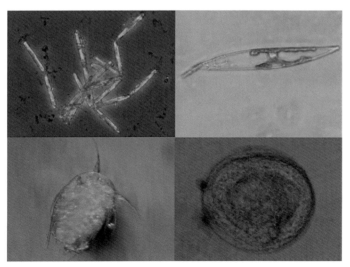

Examples of the microscopic algae (top left and right) and animals (bottom left and right) inhabiting sea ice. Larva of a crustacean (bottom left) and arrow worm egg (bottom right). Photo © Vanessa Pitusi.

Thus far, much of the biological sea ice studies from UNIS have been limited to sampling within a short time period, due to the logistical effort of reaching sites of interest. Subsequently, most datasets only cover a few days, or a couple of weeks in what is thought to be the most productive month for sea ice biology—April.

Here, the Hearts in the Ice project can help us improve our understanding of just how quickly the abundance and community of sympagic algae and meiofauna are changing through the ability to sample much more often than we ever could. Based on the samples collected in 2020, the abundance of sympagic meiofauna was lower than what has been recorded for other fjords and bays in Spitsbergen (Figure 1). The fauna was located in the lower 10 cm [4 inches] of the ice and consisted of bivalve larvae, eggs, and, potentially, nauplii. Although not much was found, the findings point toward the support of the hypothesis that sea ice is a nursery ground for larvae.

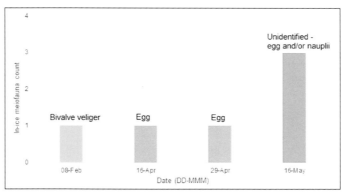

Figure 1. *Sympagic meiofauna found within the lower 10cm of sea ice in Van Keulenfjorden.*

The Hearts in the Ice project will continue to collect sea-ice samples for UNIS in 2021. Further sampling in Van Keulenfjorden will add to a slowly growing database on ice-associated sympagic life in Svalbard. With an improved sampling protocol, the Hearts in the Ice project aims to collect sea-ice samples at a higher temporal resolution,

*meaning that throughout the most biologically produc-
tive month of April, sea-ice cores will be collected every
two to three days. This should capture and provide new
insights into the development of the in-ice community in
terms of abundance and composition. We expect to be
able to pinpoint the key players in the sea-ice system in
Van Keulenfjorden and determine whether the in-ice fauna
is similar to or different from other locations, such as Van
Mijenfjorden.*

*It is crucial to map the biodiversity of sea ice in
Svalbard to understand and define the role of this unique
habitat before it is lost.*

So, how do you become a citizen scientist? How did we collect these
samples that have been so crucial to mapping biodiversity? These are
questions we have been asked often. During our time at Bamsebu, together with Joe from *Exploring by the Seat of Your Pants* (EBTSOYP), we
hosted monthly calls with schools around the world and during those
calls, several kids asked us if we needed special tools or skills to perform
the work we were doing. The answer is yes and no. It was different for
each project we undertook, but for every project, curiosity was the main
ingredient and skill we needed. For these live video/satellite calls, we had
an expert speak about a certain topic related to climate change. We would
call in with the sat phone, Joe would host via video, and we would share an
update from Bamsebu. The expert, also on video, would present on topics like technology, weather, mental and physical health, polar bears and
wildlife, our ocean, biodiversity, polar nights and auroras, food, and the
power of community. There were eight video spots for classrooms around
the world, and over the course of our year, we reached over 50,000 youth
from North and South America, India, Africa, Asia and all over Europe—it
was astounding. Connecting the kids to the experts studying change and
impact, sharing our stories from the field, and then weaving the voices
from younger generations and engaging them, and they, in turn, engaging
us, was extremely powerful and inspiring to all.

To give a more precise answer to skills involved in collecting samples:
To take ice-core samples, we would ride out onto the ice on our Lynx snowmobiles—our lifelines, next to our satellite communication equipment
and our boat. When riding out on the ice, or anywhere for that matter, we

needed to be entirely self-sufficient, which meant taking weapons for polar bear safety, adequate clothing, shovels, our handheld satellite phone, a handheld GPS, a thermos filled with hot water, and safety gear, including ice picks and a rope in the event we fell into the ice. Not to mention our ice corer (measuring 1.5 meters [5 feet]), meter scales to measure ice-core thickness and snow depth, a measuring tape, a saw for ice cores, a cutting board, four marked containers for the samples, our CastAway CTD device, and a camera. And, of course, warm, ideally waterproof, gloves since the temperature was typically around -20°C (-4°F), not taking windchill into account.

Just getting to the location to collect ice cores was an event in itself, and Ettra would always come along for the ride. All she needed was something loose that would roll around on the snow to be easily entertained for the hour.

The protocol we followed when we came back with the samples was very specific and filled three pages of text. Suffice it to say, we were diligent and took this work to heart, and we're now pros at our citizen-science work.

Various organizations have raised questions about the value of the data that citizen scientists collect. Can the results be trusted, these organizations asked, and do citizen scientists always follow the correct protocol? The consensus was that all data should be scrutinized, and the challenges remain the same whether it's collected by a scientist or a citizen scientist.

Climate change in the polar regions, and especially on Svalbard, is real. This is not just a Svalbard issue; it's a big, complex global issue. Knowledge, research, and debate are ways forward—tools that can help minimize the severity of the effects of climate change. All of us benefit from understanding the science behind these changes, and being actively involved as a citizen scientist can bring people one step closer to understanding the big picture.

The Environmental Protection Agency (EPA) has listed four key roles of citizen science:

1. ***Empowering communities*** *by encouraging citizens to take an active role in collecting, processing, analyzing, and applying information—and in encouraging new groups to participate and engage—especially those who have previously been marginalized or excluded.*

2. **Establishing ongoing monitoring**—*especially where citizens are able to collect (or have already started collecting) much larger, more detailed, thorough, and more regionally appropriate data than the agency could collect on its own.*
3. **Extending research** *to questions, areas, and topics that used to be beyond the capabilities of a government agency (i.e., new species, locations, or questions), including using citizen science to solicit various kinds of public input (such as blended research and deliberation activities).*
4. **Educating citizens** *about environmental and other issues through first-hand experiences that teach participants about both science, generally, and the particular topic of study.*

Citizen science, or community science, exemplifies the power of community to effect change and drive the cutting edge of science. By participating, citizen scientists bring their own knowledge and expertise to work in tandem with that of professional scientists, offering diverse perspectives and ground-truth data to some of the world's most difficult problems.

For our part, we at *Hearts in the Ice* wonder how much we can impact the public's curiosity about what lies beneath the ice—those teeny, tiny microscopic organizms called phytoplankton that, though they're barely visible, are responsible for more than 55 percent of the oxygen in Earth's atmosphere. We hope to keep seeding curiosity in the same way our ancestors did, before we had the internet and Google to search for answers, just like Charles Darwin did.

And not only about what lies beneath the ice, but about what lies above in the sky—the otherworldly phenomenon known as the aurora borealiz, which sways and dances and descends with lights so mysterious and bright that we could, at times, have read a page from a book by it.

The northern lights invoke such a spiritual effect that they have been featured in art, poetry, mythology, and literature. These delicate lights greatly affected even the heartiest of men, and they profoundly impacted us hearty women!

Fridtjof Nansen, a Norwegian scientist, explorer, and diplomat, was captivated by the lights. "These wonderful night effects are ever new, and never fail to captivate the soul," he wrote in 1894, on his first winter expedition. He continued: "In the north are quivering arches of faint aurora, trembling now like awakening longings, but presently, as if at the touch of a magic wand, to storm as streams of light through the dark blue of heaven—never at peace, restless as the very soul of man."

Much of the information we gathered at Bamsebu built on the pioneering work, observations, and reflections of early explorers. Nansen and his team recorded and collected data, observed the area, and took measurements for use in the areas of oceanography, marine geology, meteorology, geomagnetism, flora, fauna, and the aurora. Many of these measurements now constitute important contributions to their fields.

Another Norwegian, physicist Kristian Olaf Birkeland, made a breakthrough in auroral understanding back in 1899. Scientists had seen that the lights were a spectrum of individual lines of color, which meant that they must be given off by gases, not by solid or liquid particles on fire. But there was still no clear understanding as to the mechanism of the aurora. Birkeland's expeditions were able to deduce that the aurora was ultimately powered by the sun, thus establishing it as an "otherworldly" phenomenon.

It was decades later that it became clear that Birkeland was fundamentally correct. In the 1960s, satellites observed that there were particles in "empty" space—stellar winds and magnetic disturbances around the polar regions—just as Birkeland had deduced. His work also represented a breakthrough in our understanding of the solar system, applying electromagnetic theory outside the realms of Earth. Next time you're in Norway, look at a 200-kroner bill—Birkeland's face is on every one of them!

This is how we moved from myths surrounding the aurora to the possibility of knowledge about it—and none of it could have been done without curiosity and observation.

Svalbard—in fact, Bamsebu specifically—is the only place in the world where the daytime aurora, or cusp aurora, can be seen, and it's only visible during the polar night. This is wildly exciting to us as citizen scientists, since scientists are still working to understand the aurora, so there's a real need for more observations. The aurora is part of a larger global system, just like the oceans, and as such it has a widespread effect on our atmosphere, climate, and weather—but aside from the magnetosphere, we don't fully understand our own atmosphere.

In trying to understand the connection between the magnetosphere (the region of the atmosphere that surrounds Earth) and the ionosphere (a layer of Earth's atmosphere that's further out and which contains concentrated ions and free electrons that can reflect radio waves), old-style rocket experiments are still incredibly valuable. One way to measure aurora behavior is to release colored gas from a rocket into the aurora and document through photography where it goes. The conditions for a rocket launch have to be just right: You need clear skies at both the launch site and the monitoring location, as well as good auroral activity. NASA had us on standby for the launch of two rockets for close to a month. From 9 a.m. until 1 p.m., November 25 to December 10, we were ready to take photographs at a moment's notice, our expedition gear, safety equipment, and cameras always ready to go. The press and our NASA contacts started calling us "rocket citizen scientists," and we would get text updates and messages on our Iridium phone from NASA that looked like this:

> *"Good auroral activity today, possible launch"*
> *"Possible launch today"*
> *"Standby; waiting for improved auroral conditions"*
> *"Weather looks good at Andøya, Ny-Ålesund, clear where you are"*

We're still trying to understand this complex investigation, but here's what NASA has shared to help explain why launching rockets might help scientists understand the cusp aurora:

> *The first rocket is called CREX-2. It will launch north from Andøya Space Center on the mainland of Norway.*
> *The second is CHI, launching from Ny-Ålesund at Svalbard about fifteen to thirty minutes later. Three types of tracers will be launched. Like the smoke from a glittering fireworks display, they will drift, allowing scientists to see the unseen:*
>
> - *Barium, which is released first, reacts with sunlight and ionizes a purple-red color that drifts with the rest of the charged particles in the upper atmosphere. It elongates along the earth's magnetic field lines, likely drifting northeast.*
> - *Strontium is released second and, along with neutral barium, shows a purple blue. The strontium*

*remains neutral and shifts to a greenish-blue color
that rides along with neutral particles on the very
high-altitude wind, likely drifting northwest.*

- *At lower altitudes, small explosions release TMA
(trimethylaluminum). Its chemistry lights up white
or blue white like a glow stick, in round shapes,
then drifts with the lower-altitude neutral wind.*

This technique is one of the only ways to get these valuable measurements and has been used safely for decades, just like fireworks. By observing, measuring, and photographing the event, scientists can learn more about the structures, densities, and irregularities of the "winds" that inhabit the mysterious cusp-region aurora. We used time-lapse photography to document the whole thing—very exciting, since these wonderful night effects are ever new and never fail to captivate the soul.

As we observed the dramatic changes around us, we couldn't help but stand in awe of the wonder of this natural world and its extremities. The tides, the currents, the ice, the waves, the wind, the night sky. One day, our shoreline would be full of ice, like blocks of diamonds washed up by the brawny sea, and the next we'd have a sea full of ice as far as the eye could see. We moved with the changes.

Our fascination with every day's magical shifts made us want to applaud the early pioneers who took the first steps toward understanding why these things change as they do. Our goal was to stay passionately curious so as to better grasp how all these changes impact our climate. As self-proclaimed climate-care ambassadors, we believe it's important to keep being curious and to not just ask the questions but live them.

Today, another environmental movement is in full swing, but the damage done in the years since Carson published her epic, world-changing book is far greater than even she could have imagined. We have all watched the disasters unfold: from floods to fires to tornadoes to hurricanes, from droughts to famine to wildlife and habitat loss, species extinction, melting glaciers, shrinking icecaps, and, overall, destruction so great it has delivered us to the point of societal collapse and climate despair.

In recent years, we have seen a young woman enter the scene, a modern-day Pippi Longstocking, an old soul in an eighteen-year-old body. She was named *Time* magazine's Person of the Year in 2019—and deservedly so. Way to go, Greta Thunberg! Even at her young age, she managed to provoke a president of the United States who, during his term, set human-ity, climate-change initiatives, and the great progress made by previous administrations back by almost 100 years. Ugh!

But aside from supporting the ground swell movement that Greta has created, what is to be done? First off, scientists have found, through their research, that it will be very difficult to change the impact of climate change on landscapes, resources, people, and wildlife around the world. So how do we do it? Our *Hearts in the Ice* team believes that we need to inspire people to make changes in their daily lives. People need to feel a connection to the bigger picture and understand why their actions matter. We are convinced that encouraging people to care about the planet and the natural world will breed respect and love for what we stand to lose.

In short: We'll never change if we feel forced to, and yet we can all make a difference, and at this moment in Earth's history, each and every one of us matters.

Without further ado, here are full details of the citizen-science proj-ects we participated in at Bamsebu:

NASA—GLOBE Clouds: Arctic Cloud Observations
https://observer.globe.gov/
Key contact: Marilé Colón Robles, Project Scientist for NASA GLOBE Clouds
Researchers are interested in cloud observations, with a focus on what happens beneath the thick layers of cloud. The Arctic is known for fog-type clouds, and satellites cannot clearly see what happens below them.

They are also interested in reports distinguishing between fog and haze. Fog is a cloud that occurs on the ground, while haze is caused by aerosols or pollution in the air and gives the sky a fog-like effect.

Our third mission was to detect very thin, high clouds, such as nocti-lucent clouds. Changes observed in these cloud patterns could be related to human effects on the atmosphere.

We asked our key contact, Marilé Colón Robles, how the material we collected matters or adds value to her area of research. Here's what she said:

> *Our vantage point of the earth, from the ground looking up and into the horizon, is unique. Looking at clouds and the sky, we see the bottom of the clouds, while satellites*

see the top of the clouds. The combination of both views creates a complete story. Our view of changes is also unique and can highlight events of the changing earth that would be hard to detect using other sources of data.

NASA—AURORASAURUS: Platform for Viewing and Recording the Aurora www.aurorasaurus.org
Key contact: Dr Elizabeth MacDonald, Program Scientist, Citizen Science Strategic Working Group Lead, NASA, SMD/Heliophysics (W)

Positioned at nearly 78° north latitude, Bamsebu offers a unique vantage of the aurora, which from there is visible in the southern (rather than northern) portion of the sky. This vantage point, combined with our extended observation period of nine months, created the potential for a substantial contribution to the human understanding of the aurora borealiz, including its structure and the environmental conditions under which it occurs. We would make observations at various times, since different types of aurora occur at different times of day—but this was one science project for which we were happy to miss sleep.

The specific areas of scientific interest we studied included:

- Monitoring the cusp aurora: Visible around noon time.
- Correlation with compass: Movement in degrees would likely indicate very dynamic aurora.

Here's our contact from the Department of Physics and Astronomy at Clemson University, Professor Larsen, on why our being at Bamsebu was helpful:

The observations of the CHI rocket launch made by Sunniva and Hilde at the Bamsebu location contributed significantly to the science that we expect to get from the launch. The CHI (Cusp Heating Investigation) mission was designed to get better measurements of the heating of the neutral atmosphere in the ionosphere created by the electrical currents that result from the solar wind interacting with the atmosphere in the region where the earth's magnetic field splits and opens up to charged particles from space. The cusp location is difficult to access because of the far-north location. The rocket range on Svalbard is the only location where measurements of this type can be made from an established launch facility. Locations for supporting ground-based measurements are very limited on Svalbard, however. The fact that observations were possible from Bamsebu during the launch was fortuitous and increased the coverage of the launch substantially. We expect that the data from that location will improve the accuracy of the science data obtained from the flight.

And, we asked, how did the data *Hearts in the Ice* collected matter or add value to your area of research?

Auroras are born of the interaction between nitrogen and oxygen in Earth's atmosphere and incoming charged particles previously trapped in the magnetosphere. Geomagnetic storms, which can energize the magnetosphere with large amounts of charged particles, directly impact the creation and appearance of auroras. We aren't yet able to reliably and accurately predict space weather disturbances like geomagnetic storms, but large geomagnetic disturbances can affect the functionality of communications systems and power grids, so predicting their arrival is important.

Aurorasaurus collects ground-truth data on auroras to improve space weather nowcasting and contribute to refining models. Because citizen-scientist reports of auroras provide more localized, real-time information about where auroras are, they are also helpful in learning more about the conditions around aurora sightings themselves. As the presence of auroras indicates an influx of charged particles into our atmosphere, observing and documenting their appearances can help us understand more about impactful space weather events.

Scripps Institution of Oceanography—Fjord Phyto: Understanding Polar Fjords
https://fjordphyto.ucsd.edu
Key contact: Allison Cusick, Graduate Student (PhD), Biological Oceanography

Phytoplankton are microscopic algae that drift in the oceans. They use sunlight, nutrients, and carbon from the ocean to produce biomass in a process we know as photosynthesis. They are primary producers—basically the equivalent of plants on land. They play a critical role in drawing carbon dioxide out of the atmosphere and contribute over half of Earth's oxygen—more than plants and trees combined. But phytoplankton are at risk: Freshwater from melting glaciers negatively impacts their reproduction.

Until recently, researchers thought that phytoplankton were dead or resting during the polar night, but research conducted from 2011 to 2015 found that assumption to be false.

We conducted a weekly series of studies, using a Secchi disk underwater and a phytoplankton net.

How does what we collected matter or add value to phytoplankton research?

Phytoplankton are the key to life. They provide food and oxygen to the world. It's important to learn more about these organizms, and one way to do that is by sampling them frequently, throughout the season, to gain an understanding of which types of phytoplankton are present and how they change from month to month. Citizen-science collaborations like *Hearts in the Ice* help scientists learn more about these dynamics over time. One scientist alone couldn't manage!

British Columbia Institute of Technology (BCIT)—Visible and Thermal Drone Data
Key contact: Dr Eric Saczuk Director of RPAS Operations, Faculty and Researcher at BCIT

We captured drone data to create a map of the coastal area where we are sampling ocean water for Scripps. The drone captures both color and thermal imagery, which are analyzed for any correlation with data provided using the Secchi disks. Weather permitting, the drone flights were also timed with the overflight of the joint NASA and CNES (the French National

Center for Space Studies) CALIPSO satellite, for the purpose of mapping the distribution of phytoplankton in a near-shore marine environment.

This type of study could produce important baseline data, allowing future projects to leverage a far greater area that can be captured with a drone compared with ground sampling, and thus, someday, accurately even classify phytoplankton concentrations using satellite imagery.

Here's what Dr Saczuk had to say about how *Hearts in the Ice* matters or added value to his area of research:

> *First of all, from a more personal perspective, the data that you're collecting allows me to ascertain the effectiveness and utility of RPAS (aka drones) as a data-collection tool in a polar environment and for the purpose of climate-change research. The thermal and visible data being collected will be analyzed for its application to the quantification of surface phytoplankton concentration in a coastal Arctic region, and this would be one of the first studies of this type. It adds tremendous value to determine whether drones can be deployed into harsh polar areas to gather data related to climate change.*

The University Center in Svalbard (UNIS)
www.unis.no
Key contacts: Børge Damsgård, Professor, UNIS; Janne Søreide, Associate Professor, Marine Biology and Ecology; Vanessa Pitusi, PhD Candidate in Arctic Marine Biology

- **Insect sampling:** The scientists were interested in the diversity, distribution, and activity of insects. We collected insects until November 3 and put the "insect tent" back up in April, conducting four insect samplings in total. Most data are only from the summer.
- **Polar bear observation:** UNIS quantifies polar bear observations and conflicts with humans. They use data from a fixed station like Bamsebu to look for patterns of polar bear visits (the where, how,

who, and when of those visits) and also to understand responses when there are human/polar bear conflicts.

- **Sea-ice biological sampling:** Over the last thirty years, the duration of sea-ice cover in the Svalbard fjords has declined from an average of five months to one month. UNIS has been researching sea-ice organizms for many years, and we helped the institution during our time at Bamsebu by collecting sea ice during the spring season.

Here's what Professor Børge Damsgård at UNIS had to say about the value of our contributions:

> *Scientific samplings in polar areas are challenging, costly, and risky! Albeit the Bamsebu samplings of insects, sea-ice, and polar bear data clearly does save some work for UNIS, this is still not the most crucial added value. Over several decades, the overall trust in science has declined globally. There are obvious differences between countries, but we see more and more signs of mistrust in, for example, climate change research. One of the challenges is that most people do not feel connected to this huge global data collection. They are thus not motivated to interpret large-scale changes that, simply speaking, will decide not only the fate of polar nature but presumably the existence of the world as we know it. Citizen science is a way to close the gap between people's perceptions and scientists monitoring the climate changes. The long-term educational aspects of the Bamsebu project is thus probably the most important added value.*

Norwegian Polar Institute (NPI)—Snow-depth Study
www.npolar.no
Key contact: Dr Kim Holmén, International Director of the Norwegian Polar Institute
We conducted daily observations of sea-ice distribution in the bay, combined with weekly snow-depth and ice-thickness measurements. In particular, we observed the formation of icing layers on snow (e.g., rain during winter). A number of projects have investigated the Van Keulenfjorden

area for the effects of ongoing climate change, but these investigations have usually been of short duration and mainly during the summer seasons. *Hearts in the Ice* allowed for year-round observations that will, in turn, enhance scientists' ability to use remote-sensing data to evaluate the climatic state in the region.

The simultaneous observation of physical and biological parameters provided new data about the relationship between climate and ecozystems in the region. The Van Mijen and Van Keulen fjords are the only fjords on the west coast of Spitsbergen that still experience sea-ice formation. Year-round observations on the ground from these fjords are almost exclusively from Van Mijen, and *Hearts in the Ice* thus provided some new and unique information.

Norwegian Polar Institute (NPI)—Wildlife Observation: Polar Bears
Key contact: Dr Jon Aars, Senior Research Scientist
www.npolar.no
Data on polar bears is important to NPI. This data will help the researchers understand the potential cost of sea ice changes, from added energy expenditure to disruption of the bears' timing and success in raising cubs.

Here's what our key contact Jon Aars had to say about our contributions:

> In 2020, the spring monitor program where researchers gather data through polar bear capture had to be cancelled due to Covid-19. During this period, observations of one of our females, N26131, by Hilde and Sunniva, were of great value.
>
> Because of that, we knew she left the den with one cub in spring and that the cub was lost later in summer. Samples of polar bear scat also made it possible for us to tell which bears visited their area since we have DNA profiles on most bears that live in the area.

Norwegian Polar Institute (NPI)—Wildlife Observation: Fulmars and Plastic Ingestion
Key contact: Geir Wing Gabrielsen, Researcher, Ecotoxicology
www.npolar.no
Fulmars are pelagic seabirds that belong to the large group of the tubenoses, of which albatrosses are the best-known representatives. These birds

forage exclusively at sea—never on land and rarely even close to shore. The fulmar is a poor diver, and thus feeds on what is available. Like most tube-nosed seabirds, fulmars regularly ingest a variety of marine debris, probably mostly taken directly, either intentionally because resembling prey or unintentionally when mixed with attractive food wastes. But indirect ingestion, for instance through fish or scavenging on the guts of other dead animals, also occurs. *Hearts in the Ice* opened the stomach sacs of dead fulmars to better understand the origin and quantity of plastics they contained.

We were involved in ten projects in total, each of which had a very specific protocol for collecting data as well as its own specific tools. All of our equipment and printed protocols were given to us by the scientists we worked with, along with information on why the data we collected mattered to them and what impact it could have on our understanding of the big picture.

At Bamsebu, we were working in a very challenging environment. The dangers included frostbite, polar bear attacks, inclement and changing weather, navigating heavy seas, dealing with heavy equipment, and injury. But we were committed, dedicated, and very safe!

Changing temperatures in the Arctic are affecting everything, from the snow level to increases in avalanches to a lack of ice affecting life beneath the ice and above. The polar regions are changing. Those changes are already upon us, and they're happening faster and more drastically than most people might believe. They will compound in a domino effect, and the momentum is already increasing. The impact is enormous, life-threatening, and irreversible. Yet we still have the chance to reduce the escalation of the change. We want the world to know that we all need to pay attention. Since everything is connected, we must all make some contribution, some small change, regardless of where we live. As Fabian Dattner, founder of Homeward Bound, shared, "Mother Nature needs her daughters," and we have answered the call.

At Bamsebu, we witnessed the Arctic waking up from its long polar night. Now, it's time for all of us to wake up and get involved—for every citizen to engage with curiosity.

When we started this project, an interviewer asked us what we hoped to see on the other end of our Bamsebu stay. Here's what we said:

We hope that every single person out there understands that they matter and can make an invaluable contribution. We hope individuals will step up to their own leadership abilities, discover science projects in nature that they are passionately curious about, and become citizen scientists. Only then will we all embrace the planet!

So, find a project that needs your help and show up. Through participating, you will come to understand the changes that will impact us all. Greta is one person who has made profound changes. By working to be part of the solution, we can all be part of the solution—so we can all become a community of solutions.

Here are some last words of inspiration from our scientist collaborators:

Through Hearts in the Ice, Sunniva and Hilde have become groundbreaking pioneers in leading citizen-science-based climate change research. They are selfless, fearless, and through their sheer determination, a true inspiration for all of us to take action and reduce the negative human impact on climate change.

— Eric Saczuk, British Columbia Institute of Technology (BCIT)

Get involved! Learning is a lifelong way to feel alive. Citizen-science projects are perfect ways to learn about and contribute to things people care about. A true citizen-science project should thus be about a topic with high public awareness and, at the same time, where a tiny little contribution can still be important if enough people do it. Collecting data on a single insect or bird means nothing— knowing that there are thousands of other citizens with the same interest, doing the same thing, means a lot.

— Børge Damsgård

CHAPTER 5

TRAINING FOR THE OLYMPICS

A Day at Bamsebu

Earth and Sky, Woods and Fields, Lakes and Rivers, the
Mountain and the Sea, are excellent schoolmasters, and teach
some of us more than we can ever learn from books.
— Sir John Lubbock, The Use of Life

Before Bamsebu, we were used to our time being filled with hectic workdays and distractions all around. At Bamsebu, we had no distractions. Not even a radio. We did, however, have a series of tasks that needed to be performed each day, and they involved nature, wildlife, our projects, Ettra, and each other. There, life was filled with the most basic tasks for survival. And all that took time.

It took time to gather wood, and it took time to chop wood. It took time for the cabin to warm up. It took time to collect water or chop ice. It took time to wait for the water to boil in the morning. It took time to prepare food, clean up and wash up, and it took time to store food safely and figure out what to do with food that was about to spoil. It took time to collect research data, which often required us to wait for the weather, current, or ice conditions to change. It took time to download an email via satellite.

Time left its mark on our fresh food supply too. It was a big deal when our provisions dwindled and we'd eat the last two potatoes and tired little carrot for dinner—dinners that sometimes featured reindeer meat that we had hunted before we left, sauce, a little sauerkraut, and a glass of red wine. Luxury. We savored every bite. Life there was a wake-up call about everything we usually take for granted. We couldn't go to the store, of course, and even though Eurosupply AS (a marine food supplier) and Bring (a transport company) planned to send us shipments of provisions before Christmas, it wasn't certain a delivery would be possible. (In the end, the sea froze solid, and it wasn't possible.)

Even something as easily accessible elsewhere as drinking water was a challenge to obtain at Bamsebu, especially after the snow had melted or before any new snow had fallen. There are no natural water sources nearby, and it's an area with little snow to begin with—it's so windy that the snow doesn't stick. In periods without snow, we often found small recesses and trickles in the terrain where some snow remained after a storm. We discovered, however, that this snow was often full of sand and sediment that had blown in from the mountains and barren hilltops in the area. Even after boiling, it wasn't very appetizing.

Ensuring we had enough water became yet another survival skill we had to develop. Our solution: We had brought and filled a large intermediate bulk container (IBC) with 800 litres (211 gallons) of water from the coastal vessel MS *Nordstjernen*, the ship that dropped us off in September 2019. The water eventually froze, so when we needed drinking water, we would use an axe to chop chunks from the solid brick of ice. Without this, it would have been a challenge to get any clean water.

It was good to recognize that we didn't have a lot to spare. We took care of everything we had and preserved, brined, dried, boiled, and froze food. We ate everything we made, and we were happy for what we had. We went shopping up at Skarpsyn, especially Sunniva, and we had a lot of fun playing out how we restocked our supplies.

And all of that took time. Luckily, we had a lot of time at Bamsebu. Time was at our disposal in a completely new way, and it shaped our daily lives more than almost anything else. We didn't have a typical workday with meetings, deadlines, and spreadsheets. Instead, time at Bamsebu was marked by seasons, weather, light, darkness, a sudden storm, and the wildlife beyond our walls, all of which shaped our daily lives and determined what was urgent. Everything took time, but time was what we had. Time and peace. Deep peace.

It also took time to prepare for our winter stay—nearly three years of intense planning, to be precise. Our goals were as follows:

- Engage and inspire dialogue and action around our natural world and how to protect it.
- Make a relevant contribution to research as citizen scientists.
- Provide an interactive education platform where we host experts on subjects related to climate change and the polar regions and make this available at no cost to the general public and school kids around the world.
- Create meaningful content for social media using storytelling to inspire and inform.
- Align with partners who are part of the solution to reduce greenhouse gases.
- Live a dream and have the adventure of a lifetime.

We needed to get so much right in what felt like such a short period of time. Not only did we need to make sure we had functioning communication equipment, we also had to ensure that Bamsebu was secure, that we had enough resources for food, water, and heat, and that it was an inspiring and safe place for us to be while delivering on our goals. In short, our entire platform for *Hearts in the Ice* had to be established before we left. We spent countless late nights and weekends together, putting in an unbelievable amount of planning, sending hundreds of emails, and coordinating the logistics of our stay. We had to develop a website; connect with partners and sponsors; plan our communications strategy; sort out how we would host our monthly education calls and select the experts; secure all necessary equipment for safety and the entire stay; figure out the space and storage inside the hut, in the shed, and in Skarpsyn; protect food outside from polar bears and for Ettra; make emergency plans for polar bears, weather, and for rescue; bring all necessary science equipment and align our research projects—as well as determine how best to execute each science project.

The August before the start of our overwintering, we spent a few weeks at Bamsebu in preparation for the winter and the coming year.

It was a rather interesting time and, in fact, the first time we had been together one-on-one for more than a few days. We began to find our edges and had a few small arguments about how to do things—after all, we are two strong, smart, and opinionated women—but mostly, it was a really productive and powerful few weeks. We wanted to see what kind of storage and organization setup we would need in order to make the best use of space inside the cabin. We were like little animals, sniffing out their space to nest. We had a lot of discussions, shared thoughts and ideas, and experimented with where things would fit. We tested things like the new Evinrude engine on the boat, which allowed us to go and collect driftwood. We measured the inside space to see if two large containers would fit into a corner of the kitchen for fresh water, we tested the electric Dewalt chainsaw and how to replace the chain, we measured our space for our two coco mat mattresses in the kitchen and the living room (after all, a good night's sleep is key), we tested the MissionLINK and its satellite strength, our clothing—and we also tested ourselves. We found out how well we work together, how we communicate, and, sometimes, how we fail to communicate. We already knew we were strong enough to make this together, and we became more confident in each other skills. Together, we were super strong! We walked a lot, worked a lot, hauled a lot, and planned a lot. We were able to collect enough driftwood to stock us up for the coming months—some logs were already collected a year before—and most importantly, we had a chance to search for water sources. We already knew water might become one of our main challenges.

August is a dream month in Svalbard. At Bamsebu, we had arctic fox cubs coming in almost daily to greet us and inspect anything that was on the ground. In almost every direction, there were snow buntings, barnacle geese, guillemots, little auks, sanderlings, grey phalaropes, eider ducks, northern fulmars, gulls, pink-footed geese, arctic terns, skuas, and whooper swans. There were also dozens of belugas in the fjord—a most welcome sight. The land was dry enough to be easy to hike on; we were even able to go on a few runs. August was the perfect time to familiarize ourselves with Bamsebu and to fall completely in love with the area's diversity.

During our short, rather crazed two weeks, we also had several cruise ships come through daily. Typically, there's nobody at Bamsebu when the cruise ships do landings there during the summer months, so you can bet there was a fair amount of curiosity around who we were, what we were doing, and why we were planning to spend nine months there. We turned all the visits into opportunities to share our love of the polar regions and tell the guests about the projects we would be collecting data for, speaking to them in three languages: French, English, and Norwegian. There was one visit in particular that was very special to us: Hilde's colleagues and a ship from the Hurtigruten fleet, the MS *Spitsbergen*, sailed in with a crew from the Norwegian public broadcaster NRK to film an episode called "Svalbard, Minute by Minute"—a sort of *Slow TV*. The crew filmed the entire voyage around Svalbard, which took nearly ten days—13,390 minutes chock-full of Svalbard's history, culture, wildlife, and citizens. With their enormous camera lenses and drones, they showed the world the beauty Svalbard has to offer: its gorgeous fjords and mountains, glaciers, unique wildlife, and all the cultural history and remains of activity from centuries past.

Kari Toft, a good friend of Hilde's, was one of the hosts, and Kari and Hilde had arranged for the MS *Spitsbergen* to visit us at Bamsebu. Arne O. Holm, long-time editor of Svalbardposten and now editor of *High North News*, was one of the guides and lecturers on board who visited us here at the station. He kept a log of every day of the roundtrip voyage, and every evening, the crew filmed him reading that day's recollections. On the final day, he chose the topic of Arctic women, inspired by, among other things, his visit to Bamsebu:

> The "modern" over-winter stay, if one can call it that, has fascinated me for a long time because the transition from a normal life to a trapping station is so much greater today than it was in the past when winter residents would move from one remote village in northern Norway to an equally remote village on Svalbard.
>
> In earlier days, the life they moved away from was pretty much the same as the life they moved to. The struggle for food could be just as hard for a fisherman from Andøya as for a reindeer hunter in Austfjordneset. Those who pull up roots today and set out on the untamed land are leaving behind a completely different life—a life with well-stocked grocery shelves in contrast with spending a season without access to shopping centers or flight departures. This is about turning off the TV and social media in

exchange for complete silence, in exchange for the absence of visual and other sensory input other than what the natural world can offer.

But then, this is exactly what Hilde and Sunniva wish to experience. They are about to face the break they have desired for several years. Never before, if one is to believe the oracle Per Kyrre Reymert, have two women spent an entire winter alone on Svalbard. History is still being written for the future historians and statisticians of Svalbard.

I have known Hilde for twenty years, and I know that she will succeed and enjoy it. Sunniva has a list of accomplishments that makes her better prepared than any man for a year in the wilderness at nearly 78 degrees north. If anyone wonders if I envy them, the answer is an unconditional yes.

Hilde and Sunniva will manage it, but they have made a bold choice. To embark on a nine-month expedition requires an endless list of equipment and shopping lists. But there is so much more. The psychological backpack needs to be stocked as well. After the trip has begun, it's too late to clean up what you're leaving behind.

To seek solitude in Svalbard during the dark part of the year isn't just about bidding farewell to civilization for nine months. It's first and foremost about daring to meet yourself.

Only the bravest among us dare to do that.

The program featuring this trip to Svalbard aired on NRK TV from January 31 until February 9, 2020, and was seen by millions of viewers. That was when many Norwegians were introduced to *Hearts in the Ice* and the two women who had chosen to spend nine months at Bamsebu.

Closer to the start of our winter stay, we continued to prepare by taking three trips to Bamsebu on Hilde and Steinar's forty-foot boat, *Liefdefjord*. Even in a boat of that size, you feel tiny during a trip to Bamsebu. Sea conditions, regardless of the size of the boat, are always unpredictable in the Arctic, so we made sure to plan our trips for times when the weather was more agreeable. We got lucky and ended up with mostly good conditions each time. These trips were critical for our preparation—on each trip, we brought along two small boats attached to the boat in the back with towlines. These smaller, heavy-duty plastic "river boats" and an Evinrude outboard motor ended up being vital pieces of our winter mission. We used them to collect driftwood and saltwater samples for analyzing phytoplankton and to explore the fjord, and they were also critical in case we ever needed to get help from a passing ship—so we took good care of them. The boat's towline was critical, the most secure way to leave and approach the shore in bad weather *and* in slush. We didn't go too far out into open waters when we were gathering data or collecting wood and provisions. For example, for one late delivery of goods, we had to be prepared to pull ourselves out and reel ourselves in again in heavy swells. The boat was safely attached to a buoy when the weather was bad, and it bobbed up and down like a little cork when the sea was choppy.

But even with all the time we spent preparing and familiarizing ourselves with Bamsebu, there's nothing like the moment you actually land somewhere, the moment when the wheels touch down. It took time to get used to working together, living together in a small space, storing and rotating our food, keeping the hut warm, making sure we had enough fresh water—all part of our new normal. We had to get the hang of things, and we both had to work to get on the same page. The first few weeks involved a lot of important discussions, and some tears were shed during the process. But we hit the ground running. We were living with purpose—an overarching theme that carried us through the hard times.

It was important for us to get going with gathering data for the researchers and our various projects. The gear took up a lot of space, both under our beds and outside in containers, so we had to keep organized and remember where everything was. In late September 2019, after just a couple of weeks at Bamsebu, we held our first virtual classroom call with Joe Grabowski and *Exploring by the Seat of Your Pants*, a non-profit that brings science, exploration, adventure, and conservation to classrooms around the world through virtual meetings with leading experts in the field. It was really fun to share our story with thousands of kids. We would take part in three of these calls every single month, while introducing classrooms around the world to experts on a wide range of topics. We shared our insights and observations with the children and told them what we were up to in the Arctic, and why.

Just a few weeks in, we had already had an overwhelming number of new experiences, and we were working hard to maintain a regular blog, photograph each part of our journey, and line up regular communication with our partners, sponsors, and educators. It felt like an endless list of tasks to fulfillll; at times, it felt a bit insurmountable, but by putting one foot in front of the other and completing one thing at a time, we developed a good flow with our projects and routine in our daily lives. Slowly but surely, this became our new normal, our everyday routine. We learned to shape our days so that they were in harmony with everything around us—and we enjoyed it! Which doesn't mean things weren't hard: There were tons of challenges, from the size of our cabin to the location to learning how to cook in the cabin's primitive kitchen. But we found that dealing with the various challenges of our new life became much easier as we established our routines.

This is just one way that developing a routine was key to our survival and our physical and mental health. Even outside of Bamsebu, routines allow for rhythm and structure and can motivate you and make you feel like you've accomplished something. We developed a routine for everything, from getting up, lighting the stove, boiling water, making breakfast, and making the bed to personal hygiene, working out, getting dressed for our activities, and simply getting out of the cabin. Routines helped keep us on target with basic tasks, even if the weather was bad, it was pitch-black outside, or we were tired.

Knowing how influential a routine could be in creating a good mood, we kept practices for sleeping and eating, both important aspects of mental and physical well-being. A routine that includes moving the body has saved many a weary, forlorn, hopeless soul. We thought back to the early explorers of the Arctic, the Antarctic, and places in between, and how often we had heard their recipe for survival: When you're down, get outside and move! When you're dark, chase the light. Writings from early survivors of the polar night point to a clear fact: Doing nothing can sink you into depression, cabin fever, and mental instability, which can lead to death. We knew, from day one, that our daily rhythm would be vital to our health and survival and that we had to make the best of what we had inside and outside our little hut.

The daily tasks and routines we maintained helped us to feel a sense of normalcy, but some were also about survival in a more literal sense— such as checking the weather when we got up and making sure everything outside was tied down before we went to bed, just in case. If it was really windy, it would be harder to keep the stove going and the cabin warm, which would mean we needed more firewood inside. Freezing temperatures and gale force winds are not a good combination for an old trapper's cabin. We chopped a lot of wood in the autumn, but wood chopping remained an ongoing, nearly daily task throughout our stay, as did dealing with raw and downright wet firewood since, ideally, firewood should be chopped at least a year in advance.

If you've seen photos of where we are—Van Keulenfjorden, in the northwestern part of South Spitsbergen National Park—you will know that there is nothing but open sea, mountains, and endless Arctic tundra. During the winter, it's completely covered in white and so dark outside that our vision was limited to the beam of light from our headlamps, which reached 60 to 70 meters (200 to 230 feet) max. Beyond that, uncertainty crept in, which is one reason we carried weapons and signal flares. Carrying a weapon every single day became part of our routine, and we also had to get used to the idea that if it came down to it, we would have to use that weapon as a matter of life or death. As a hunter and having lived in Svalbard for decades, Hilde was far more familiar with using weapons. Sunniva had less experience but had taken firearm training in Canada before the expedition.

We ate well and were both focused on staying strong and fit so that we could handle our physical tasks, like pulling our boat ashore after launching it to collect phytoplankton and saltwater for our citizen-science projects: *one, two, three, pull!* Or lifting logs: *one, two, three, lift!* Or chopping wood or holding Ettra back when she spotted a reindeer.

When we worked out inside, we had light, but less than 20 square meters (215 square feet) of space. We trained five days a week, and everything we used for our workouts was either stored in a crate under the bed or attached to the ceiling or a wall for easy hanging when not in use. We had gymnastic rings in the kitchen (no joke!), a pull-up bar, a slackline (also in the kitchen), foam rollers, rubber bands, balls, yoga blocks, push-up handles, and also a skipping rope that we couldn't quite find space to use.

And perhaps as important as all of our equipment was the music we trained and stretched to. We even had a hammock in the kitchen. Our music was always random and included Norwegian artists, Motown, soft rock, 70's, 80's, R&B—you name it, we had it all on hard drives. We maximized the usable floor space by shoving the table against the couch and rolling out two yoga mats—and this was where the real training happened. Our workouts included two sets of six Undersun resistance band exercises, push-ups, pull-ups, sit-ups, and then stretches, and the space was so limited that we had to do all this simultaneously and in synchrony. We became "Olympic champions" in synchronized exercising! "Synchronized stretching must be an Olympic sport!" we would insist as we stretched, legs in sync at right angles. In fact, we're so convinced our synchronized stretches will catch on that we plan to make instructional videos soon. Right, left, up, down. It must be taught!

As for exercising outdoors: Running outside in this vast landscape is completely magical! During the months when you can actually see them, the mountains and fjords look like a theater set in all possible light conditions and variations. We ran on the ice for several months too. On one run, we ran into a female polar bear and two large two-year-old cubs, almost as big as the mother. The cubs were very curious. We caught a glimpse of them on our way back to the cabin, and though they were moving toward us, we got home and managed to maintain a safe distance. They visited the cabin that day, and we were both glad to be back inside. When you're out on foot and you run into a polar bear, you feel vulnerable and small. Rule number one: You must never try to run away from a polar bear.

During the Arctic night, our runs and our routes were naturally limited. Even though we had good Moonlight headlamps, there was a lot we couldn't see. We would run laps up and down on the flattest parts of the tundra, so as not to invite surprise encounters—things like polar bears at the top of a hill or below a highpoint—and carry night vision binoculars when we ran or walked. Our runs would typically last about thirty minutes, during which our eyes were constantly busy, our heart rates reached as high as 176, and our calves and thighs burned.

We were also more vulnerable to changes in the weather while running, since we would wear relatively light clothing in below-zero temperatures. Our base layer for running consisted of:

- ✓ Wool tights over base layer
- ✓ Wool skirt over base layer
- ✓ Two pairs of socks
- ✓ Running shoes
- ✓ Gaiters
- ✓ Down jacket
- ✓ Waist belt with holster and signal pistol
- ✓ Weapon for polar bear safety

- ✓ Hat
- ✓ Neck gaiter
- ✓ Goggles
- ✓ Headlamp
- ✓ Ettra
- ✓ Positive attitude and motivation

There were lots of reindeer around, which made for a good workout for Ettra and Hilde, who was better at holding Ettra back since she weighs more than Sunniva. The reindeer were curious, found Ettra entertaining, and liked to tease her. They seemed to know exactly how far her leash would reach and pass just beyond her range. For the most part, she didn't let them get the best of her, but once in a while, she would lunge at them suddenly, and the reindeer would run about 50 meters (165 feet) away before returning later for another round of action.

Ettra needed a couple of daily walks, and we did too. She gave us that extra little push to go outside, regardless of the conditions—except for a few days during the harshest Arctic nights when it wasn't a good idea to go out. It was simply too dangerous; even Ettra didn't want to go out! She played a big part in our mental health and daily routines, and she satisfied our need for affection since she loved being cuddled, petted, and groomed, and she loved to spend time with us. She has a wonderful disposition and was eager to please, adapting easily to our habits and commands and doing what she was told inside the cabin. And though she's a very powerful dog with a strong prey drive and instincts, she's also a little lazy and couldn't be bothered unless the wildlife was very close by. All in all, she's a very quiet and peaceful dog, without a single ounce of aggression in her, and we certainly never heard a peep from her—no whining, no complaining. Ever.

However, for whatever reason, not a lot of Arctic dogs are actually good at warning of incoming polar bears, so we weren't at all sure if Ettra would. Then it happened: a sharp bark from Ettra. It was the dark, early-morning hours of November 12, and an enormous male polar bear had startled her while she was sleeping outside. We later estimated that he weighed somewhere between 600 and 700 kg (1,323 and 1,764 lbs) based on his 62-cm (2-foot) pads.

It was the first time we had heard her bark. We rushed to the door, but by then, the polar bear was already out of sight, scared away by a terrified dog and perhaps also by the sounds we made rushing out of the cabin. It was completely dark outside. Ettra is a very deep sleeper, and after inspecting the tracks around her, we assumed he actually sniffed her. After that day, she'd always warn us when there was a polar bear nearby, and that was absolutely worthy of strong praise. *"Good girl, Ettra! Good Ettra!"*

One regular outing that was never pleasant or warm was a trip outside to answer nature's call, which, before the ice came, meant walking down to the waterline. It's one thing to go when it's windy and rainy, but quite another when it was 30 below zero (-22°F) with a biting wind. It was always a bit of an expedition: We would have to put all of our clothes on, make sure we had a flare gun, a revolver and headlamp, and walk to the waterline, only to have to take most of our clothes off again. It was such a hassle. Many times, during storms, we'd pee in a bucket in the hallway instead. When the ice formed and we didn't want to leave any organic waste on it, we started to use the outhouse. It was a nice little outdoor toilet with a Styrofoam seat. Pure luxury—not quite. It was a small wooden shed that also housed all of our tools, extra food, spare parts, miscellaneous items, some fuel, a large Dewalt outdoor light, a few saws, an axe, and some of our science equipment. And on the floor, a small wooden box with a black Styrofoam seat and a slat of wood to cover it when not in use. Inside that wooden box was a yellow bucket filled with double-lined bio bags. We burned the toilet paper so that only organic waste remained in the bucket, and that organic waste froze immediately. Twice during the course of the winter, we took "little yellow" over to the other bay north of the cabin and tossed the clump of frozen toilet waste into a crack in the ice. No plastic and no paper. By the time the ice receded in the spring, we were so comfortable using our luxurious outhouse that we never quite managed to return to the waterline.

Our routine was easily impacted and dictated by natural events, wildlife, and weather—any day or night could bring a polar bear visit, a reindeer outside the window, foxes, or birds. Depending on the time of year, we would also prioritize things like photographing the northern lights, a snowmobile trip under the midnight sun, a ski trip in our backyard, a kayak trip to collect phytoplankton when the sea was calm, or simply standing outside the cabin and taking it all in. It wasn't always easy to go to bed! We felt like little kids, never quite done with exploring the day. There was never a dull, ordinary day at Bamsebu, mostly because we both like to have fun and there was so much weather and so many polar bears to keep track of.

That being said, it was our routine that saved us: through the long, dark, seemingly endless polar night, through the sheer lack of stimulation from the phone never ringing, through no news ever arriving from the outside world (or at least, arriving very seldom), and through the honest truth that just being there in that white winter wonderland had its challenges, both mental and physical.

Here's a sample of the daily routine that saved us:

7:00 a.m. (ish): The first one up, usually Hilde, would start the heating process. She would get the fire going and start the slow, cumbersome process of getting some heat inside so we could live and work. We would check the weather. We had a weather station out on the roof with a monitor inside; the key things to check were the wind speed, temperature, windchill, and temperature inside the cabin. We would check the area around the cabin for wildlife (mainly polar bears) and bring Ettra in, and she would jump up on Hilde's bed. Ettra always slept either in the entryway or outside. Her fur is thick enough to withstand all sorts of weather, and she always preferred to sleep outside, even when it was -30°C (-22°F). But she didn't like the wind, even in the summer. If there was a storm, or if we had recently had a polar bear visit, she would sleep in the entryway, where it was almost as cold as it was outside.

8:00 a.m.: It was usually still too cold to move our arms out from under the comforter to type on the computer or read. We would put water on for coffee and tea. If there was any light outside, we would open the outside wooden shutters—and going outside to open them would involve getting fully dressed, with a safety-belt revolver, signal pistol, and all. While we were outside, we would check again for wildlife or tracks. We would put Ettra on a long leash while we opened the shutters, and she would sniff the perimeter and have a pee. Then it was back inside.

8:30 a.m.: Coffee and tea in thermal cups with lids.

10:00 a.m.: We would feed Ettra and make cereal and oatmeal for breakfast, then we would usually check email or curl up with a good article or book and our hot drinks before rising and shining completely. We would talk about any "news" we had received or dreams we could remember, or things we wanted to do that day, given the wind and weather. Lying about 3 meters (10 feet) apart in our respective beds, we would have to talk in slightly louder voices than normal.

11:00 a.m.–12:00 p.m.: The temperature in the cabin would be starting to become bearable. We would already be busy working on communication, emails, the blog, and our projects, often under the comforter. We often felt that we had nothing going on except for what was front and center staring right at us: this Arctic landscape. But in truth, we were connecting with a network of students, climate change experts, and science partners, and we had press requests and more to deal with, so we were often busy, with no shortage of emails to reply to. One of the best parts of email was that we got to turn it on and off. We would open up our laptops in the morning and download all of our emails, then work offline, with no pinging noises in the background. Regardless of the time of year and the weather, at this point we would also plan the rest of the day's activities. We would be gearing up for our science projects—what to do and when—and planning that day's exercise. Would we run, ski, or kayak? Sometimes we would also take in a thirty-minute yoga session through our laptops. Every morning, we had to see what the weather was like and what we had scheduled in terms of school calls, interviews, and meetings before we could decide on the day's activities.

1:00 p.m.: This was the bewitching hour when we would put on all of our clothes to head out for an extensive period of time. Regardless of the weather, we would go on a walk or a run with Ettra before working out. We even ran when it was -20°C (-4°F), as long as it wasn't windy. The coldest run we ever had was on a -19°C (-2°F) day, when the wind picked up after we set out. Our fingers nearly froze off.

2:00 p.m.: Lunch. We would have worked up an appetite by this time, so we might indulge in the greatest luxury of our stay: a smoothie with green kale and spirulina powders, almond meal, beet powder, frozen fruit, protein powder, almond milk, and chia, flax, and hemp seeds. It was such a treat to have solar and wind power to fire up a blender once in a while. Otherwise, we would have crispbread with mackerel in tomato sauce or cheese, crackers with cheese, a nice bowl of soup, or—if we had them—fresh vegetables like tomatoes, avocado, or cucumber.

3:00 p.m.: Time to go outside to collect research data. Depending on the time of year, this might mean flying a drone, sampling ice cores or phytoplankton, taking saltwater temperatures, observing and recording animal life, collecting insects, observing clouds, or photographing the northern lights. All this would include quite a bit of coordination: getting equipment together, making sure we had fresh batteries if we were flying the drone, etc. Given that we had such a small space with a lot packed into it, there was always a bit of running around to do when we needed to find something, like a battery charger. We also had other jobs to complete in the afternoon, like chopping wood; gathering ice, snow, or water; and emptying the organic waste bucket into the sea. We would make sure that we had brought in food for dinner and had sufficient supplies of food, water, and firewood inside for possible rough weather. We would also empty the water container from the power source and sort through our paper, glass, and metal waste. Life was busy but extremely gratifying and purpose-driven.

6:00 p.m.: We always got a workout in before dinner, so we would transition from our snowmobile trip or whatever else the afternoon brought us into our home gym and workout studio. This involved pulling out our yoga mats and our bag of TA2 Undersun resistance bands, putting on our training clothes and running shoes, and working out with Undersun founder James Grage on the laptop for roughly thirty minutes, one body part at a time. We never quit, and we would each cheer the other on. Of course, we didn't always feel like working out, but we would show up, get into our workout clothes, and get started anyway. It was always such a bonus mood lifter if one of us was feeling less than motivated or sleepy. Since it's dark for three months, it's easy to feel like you never fully wake up—so says Sunniva.

7:00 p.m.: Satellite call with classrooms and students all over the world through Exploring by the Seat of Your Pants and host Joe Grabowski. We would use our satellite phone to call into Zoom meetings where the students would be watching on video along with Joe and an expert we had invited to join us. Calling into Zoom is not as easy as it sounds. For some reason, the automated voice never seemed to recognize the codes we entered for the meeting room, so we would re-enter the code again and again and again until we had to hang up and try again. We would typically have to redial in at least three or four times during the course of a class or webinar; our record was forty-seven attempts during one session. It was always good to have the ever-professional Joe, who knew us and the project well, to keep the whole thing going and take over automatically when our service got dropped. It was a true test of patience. Even so, the format of the calls was always spirited and extremely engaging since Joe is a master host. We would be introduced first, so students knew who we were and exactly where we were and that we were on satellite. We would share an update, and then our guest expert would share a presentation for approximately fifteen minutes before the students had a chance to ask questions of either us or the expert. They had great questions that often stumped the expert, and the sessions were always rewarding and inspiring.

8:00 p.m.: Dinnertime! Always made with great effort and care. Of the two of us, Sunniva would make the more creative dinners. She loves to use words from French restaurants, so it would always sound like we were enjoying exotic spices and the "special of the day" right there at Bamsebu. Dinner was always a highlight of the day: We would set the table, light a candle, and share a glass of wine if we had any. Cooking became more of a challenge during the periods when we were out of vegetables and other important ingredients, but dinnertime was always good, and we always appreciated what we had.

10:00 p.m.: If we had planned for it, and the communication technology was working well, we would have some phone time with people involved in the project or with family. Regardless of the weather, we would get dressed and head outside for a short walk to get some air and let Ettra do her business. We would bring night vision binoculars, headlamps, safety gear, and our Lynx goggles. After our walk, there might be time for a video. We would always close the shutters for the night, regardless of the time of year. Bedtime would typically be anywhere from 11 p.m. to 1 a.m. Once in a while, we would watch a movie we had on a hard drive, but sometimes the northern lights would have us outside for hours, often until 2 a.m. Then, at some point, it was time to call it a day.

CHAPTER 6

SILENCE

QUIET IS HARD TO FIND

The intuitive mind is a sacred gift and the rational mind is a faithful servant.
We have created a society that honors the servant and has forgotten the gift.
— Albert Einstein

We were careful to keep our souls connected to exactly where we were, in the high north. We had no room for negativity, irritation, or anger—they did show up in very small ways, but rarely. The choices we made and the things we told ourselves were critical to our mental well-being; in a situation like that, they really could mean life or death. Listening to the thoughts we fed ourselves bred wisdom in our responses, but for that process to unfold, we had to listen, and the only way we found to do that was to be quiet. Let the silence speak.

We were tucked away in our small cabin, where the only noises were the subtle ones we made and the sometimes less subtle ones that nature made: the sound of the cabin creaking under the pressure of a storm or snowdrifts whipping against the walls and windows in a cloud of white. The sound of cold, fresh saltwater waves or drowsy, murmuring waves, heavy with sea ice. The call of the snow bunting in springtime, or the geese cackling nervously when a fox—or perhaps we—were nearby. The lone howl of an arctic fox up at the foot of the mountain or a grouse calling out for a mate. The sound of wood crackling in the stove, Ettra's chain clinking when she moved or our talking, singing, or laughing.

But despite these sounds, inevitably, silence made its way into every little open space. The quiet was unlike anything we had known—a peace that blanketed us the same way the snow blanketed the landscape and mountains around us. Softly. Fully. Completely.

SUNNIVA ON SILENCE

Only when I understood that I had a primal need for silence was I able to begin my search for it many years ago—and there, deep beneath a cacophony of humming and buzzing and thoughts, music, machinery, and iPhones, it lay in wait for me. Silence. The world's secrets are hidden inside it.

It turns out silence can also be unsettling. Think of the times you've meditated and a minute has felt like an hour, and you've done nothing but think about thinking and how you're not supposed to think for just one darn minute.

Think of the two-minute silence on Remembrance Day or the minute's silence at a football game as a mark of respect for someone who has died. Both for Hilde and me, there was also the minute of silence we'd experience on Zodiac cruises when, deep into the Antarctic or Arctic, we would cut the engines and sit in silence with our guests for one whole minute. Occasionally at such times, there's someone who just can't cope with the power that arises from the collective silence, and they rustle or speak to break it.

You can't just switch off your thoughts. It takes work.

On my long, slow slog to the South Pole back in '92 and '93, I had close to two-and-a-half months of moving in silence, with just the wind and my thoughts for company. It was my first true, deep experience of a quiet that I, too, had initially dreaded and worked hard to distract myself from. I was thirty years old and young and fit, or so I thought, but I suffered for much of the trip—almost all 1,500 km (930 miles). I had knots in my neck, sore hips, an achy lower back, tendonitis in my ankles, bronchitis, cracked fingers, and bloody, blistered lips. Yet, despite being in so much physical pain every single day, I began to find myself getting lost in my thoughts, floating on a distant cloud or a snow crystal. It was the deepest form of meditation possible without falling asleep. Talk about being in the moment.

"It is what the sailor holding a tight course feels when the wind whips through her hair . . . . what the painter feels when the colors on the canvas begin to set up a magnetic tension with each other, and a new thing, a living form, takes shape." These words were written by Hungarian-American psychologist Mihaly Csikszentmihalyi to describe the state of "flow," a condition of heightened focus, productivity, and happiness that we intuitively understand and hunger for. Csikszentmihalyi found that people in this flow state can engage so completely in what they're doing that they lose track of time. All sense of self recedes—and at the same time, they are able to push beyond their own limits and abilities. Indeed, some of life's most fulfilllllling moments can occur when a person's body or mind is stretched to capacity in this flow state. It's in this flow state that deep peace and inner silence are found.

There in the stark interior of Antarctica—all 14 million square kms (5.4 million square miles) of her—I began to find comfort in her quiet emptiness. I had pushed beyond my limits and abilities. I had surrendered. It was a moment of grace, peace, buckets of tears, and a silence that I will never forget. It was like coming home.

If you can let the silence be a white canvas on which you toss only that which serves you well, that is a true sign of strength.

But oh, those voices in our heads!

At Bamsebu, we would take daily walks, and when we walked in the dark, our thoughts wouldn't always be rational. In the dark, fear can creep into the silence—or, as American author Wayne Dyer calls it, that "gap between our thoughts." We made it a daily practice to meet our fears, one thought at a time, make friends with them, thank them for visiting, and then send them on their way.

When you strip away noise, it's easier to let go of the day-to-day, settle your thoughts, and listen. Doing this collectively and in community with others through either a yoga class or a group meditation makes the silence even more valuable. If you're restless, you can sense the stillness of those around you; other people's stillness can remind you of your goals and encourage you to sit still and try again. It takes practice, practice, practice.

Many cultures around the world have traditional practices and celebrations designed to help them reconnect with the *core* of who they are. We could call these "regenerative forces"—rituals that serve to revive people—and silence is often central to them. Some indigenous people of the American Southwest believe that to cultivate wisdom and character, you must develop the capacity to be fluid like water, warm like fire, and solid like a mountain, or you will suffer soul loss or some disconnection from what is meaningful and life-giving.[6] The symptoms of disconnection and soul loss can look like apathy, anxiety, depression, emptiness, confusion, self-doubt, irritation, restlessness, or numbness.

Our ancestors needed silence to listen for encroaching danger, be it wildlife or storms, but today, things are different. With the advent of technology and the accelerated speeds at which we can now connect with each other, opportunities to actively listen to silence and the sounds that only nature can produce have become rare. If we want silence, we have to seek it out, but it's worth it. Through silence and through pausing, we can rediscover the things that bring us joy and the wisdom of our intuitive selves.

For at least three months, time at Bamsebu isn't driven by sunsets, sunrises, or any other external markers. It's easy to get lost in that kind of time—which is why we had to stick to our routines and tasks and avoid getting too lost. But routines aside, what a gift it was to sit there in that quiet space, in that remote Arctic landscape, and feel and listen to the greatest teacher there is: the wildness of Mother Nature. Open spaces like Antarctica and the Arctic—and, specifically, Bamsebu, at 77.55 latitude, 15.06 longitude—are geographies of possibility. Living there felt like we were living in complete, perfect stillness.

A thud outside our cabin jolts us out of bed. Ettra is lying on the living room floor, so we know it's not her. On go our boots, down jackets, and

---

[6] Angeles Arrien, *The Second Half of Life: Opening the Eight Gates of Wisdom* (United States: Sounds True, 2009).

headlamps, and we grab the flare gun and rifle. Somewhat cautiously, we open the door and creep outside just a few meters into a corner of the entryway and quickly turn on the floodlight. We take a peek around to the food storage area. Nothing. Our pulses are rising: That sure sounded like a polar bear climbing onto the roof. We circle the cabin. No polar bears. No tracks in the snow. Strange.

Back inside, we spot the culprit: a can of sparkling water that had frozen, exploded, and jumped off the top shelf and onto the floor.

At Bamsebu, our senses were highly attuned to the environment, always listening for animals—polar bears and reindeer—crunching by in the snow. We heard the howl of the wind as it screamed past our stovepipe and shook the walls of our uninsulated cabin. With ice floes so tightly packed together we heard them breathe in and out as they labored toward the shore in a pool of slushy ice. We felt the weight on our shoulders of pulling a 400-kg (880-lb) boat and heard its sluggish drag across the snow *One, two, drag . . .*

We heard ourselves, out of breath, doing our *Hearts in the Ice* workout.

We heard Ettra groan with delight as she splayed across the cool wooden floor with all four legs in the air.

And we heard the wire from the radio antenna slap across the wood— an incessant slap that constantly reminded us of the 30 m/s (67 mph) wind.

We heard the cycles of change from day to day, season to season.

And we heard the silence.

We heard the beat and pulse of Mother Nature.

She breathed and roared and cried and whispered.

And what we couldn't hear, we experienced.

We couldn't hear the sound of a shooting star.

Or the dance of the northern lights.

And though we knew they were out there, somewhere, we couldn't hear the sounds of the nearest town of Longyearbyen, 140 km (87 miles) away or the Iridium satellite orbiting above at 27,360 kph (17,000 mph)— spinning round the whole earth in just 100 minutes.

We found the sweet sound of silence and peace of mind. In this quiet space, there was room for us to welcome in every friend, loved one, and family member. We held space for so many of our followers and for you reading this book. Our work is a lens through which to view and experience the world, but ultimately, the goal is to make living itself, the act of being fully alive, one's vocation! The greatest creative challenge is the struggle to be the architect of one's own life: to live with intention but also in the full knowledge that, ultimately, nothing can be planned or anticipated, that any blueprint can only go a certain way toward predicting the outcome of something as complex as a human life.

So how does one go about becoming the architect of their own life?

It's worth noting that thought is very powerful: Whatever you think about expands (more on that in the next chapter). Also worth noting: Every crisis in our world has brought with it great change and opportunity. But in order to find the purpose, you first have to find your silence, your inner peace.

Humans are social creatures, unable to function alone, so being accessible is a good thing. But it's also important to be able to turn off your phone, sit down, and say nothing. To shut your eyes, breathe deeply a couple of times, and at least attempt to think about something other than what you normally think about. Original thought is a gift.

You don't need special techniques to experience silence or to simply pause. You don't need to take a course or journey all the way to Bamsebu. You can find silence anywhere, any time—it's right in front of your nose. You can create it for yourself as you walk, prepare food, or merely focus on your breathing. Sure, we're all part of the same world, but you carry with you at all times the great potential wealth of becoming an island unto yourself, even if just for a time. To move slowly from one place to another has become a privilege that many people can't afford because they need to get from point A to point B quickly. But whenever possible, we can try to slow down and make the morning last.

We have found that silence brings enhanced creativity—it's a space you can access to solve the big problems and find solutions for things you're grappling with.

The past year and a half of pandemic have shaken many to their core, leaving them isolated or always together, and perhaps jobless. As many people struggle to adapt to this unknown territory, even the challenges thrust upon us by Covid-19—including quarantine, working from home, and the lack of access to regular services like kids' activity centers, cinemas, gyms, and schools—could give us a renewed sense of purpose and serve to anchor the very reason we are all here:

> To love each other,
> to problem-solve together,
> and to be of service for the greater good.

We are all in this together, and that will make us stronger.

CHAPTER 7

EXPEDITION BEHAVIOR

Wilderness is the Great Teacher

*The quest for certainty blocks the search for meaning. Uncertainty
is the very condition to impel man to unfold his powers.*
— Erich Fromm

HILDE

"Watch out for the wave!" I roared through the deafening wind and sea. Little did we know that a summer outing to Gipsvika Bay in my rigid inflatable boat, *Wanny*, would be a true test of our mettle for our upcoming winter stay. It was summer 2018, the summer before we would begin our stay at Bamsebu, and I was standing waist-deep in water in my immersion suit, calling out frantically to Sunniva. We had been on a magical trip to the Von Post Glacier and stopped outside Villa Fredheim where, some seventy years ago, the intrepid Arctic woman Helfrid Nøis had spent many winters with her husband, Hilmar, introducing a new era in the Svalbard trapper's life by transforming a trapper station run by men for decades into a warm and cozy home with curtains, tablecloths, flowers, and growing herbs. On our return trip, we ate our packed lunches at Bjonahavna. The wind picked up a bit before we began the final leg of our trip home, around Tempelfjellet (Temple Mountain) to Gipsvika. Tempelfjellet will take your breath away, rising out of the sea like a temple—but we couldn't bask in its glory for too long. Within seconds, a calm and unbelievably beautiful day turned into a windy afternoon with the waves picking up quickly.

Weather changes in minutes in the Arctic. We had a buoy in the bay outside the hut we were visiting, but it seemed unnecessary to attach the bow of the boat to the rope at the buoy and slowly haul us backwards to the beach. The waves seemed manageable. The moment we came to the sandy beach, the waves were bigger than interpreted, and the stern of the boat was quickly thrown around. Waves crashed down on us and our boat, which was now sideways and capsized at the waterline. What looked like a harmless wave threw the boat around and filled it with water—tons of water. Wanny's hull is heavy and V-shaped, and it quickly dug itself into the beach's sand.

The sea continued its assault, and water filled the boat until it finally rolled sideways. We fought like crazy to secure the rope to the bow while screaming to one another, "Be careful!" The carabiner had to be secured to the bow of the boat in order to pull the boat out from the shore and out to the open water to the buoy and anchor. With such enormous forces in action, we could easily have been caught under the boat, pulled underwater, or dragged out to sea by the strong tides. The waves kept crashing, and it seemed hopeless. We were exhausted. I had one knee pressed against the hull and a foot well anchored in the sand. How much can one leg bone withstand?

But little by little, with both of us hanging onto the mooring rope, we finally managed to secure the carabiner to the rope on the bow. The rope was attached to the buoy and the anchor out at sea. We pulled the rope as hard as we could, at the same time, with all our weight pushing against the boat. First, we dislodged it from the beach—we got it out, bow first, until there was water under the keel. Out! Out! Slowly but surely, we managed to rotate the bow, and the sea gradually lost its grip. The boat was loaded with several tons of water, and the ocean kept tossing more in, wave upon wave of it while the boat rolled sideways in the pounding surf; but inch by inch, we managed to coax it out of the sand. *There! Now it's loose!* Even though the boat was still full of water, it was possible with hard work to pull it out toward the buoy. Our pulley system was finally in place. The boat was fully capable of floating full of water.

We had misjudged the waves and hadn't used the anchoring system we had set up the day before. Had we attached the boat to the buoy and anchor with the bow facing out toward the sea before descending to the shoreline, this would never have happened. Thankfully, we weren't hurt, and we saved the boat. Sore and exhausted—and with one Iridium phone and one mobile phone drowned in saltwater and much of what we had taken with us soaking wet—we managed to get back to the cabin where we fired up the stove and processed what had happened. We had learned a lesson—conditions can look calmer out on the open sea than they are at the beach—and we now saw the advantage of actively using the mooring rope during our trips out to sea and in toward land. We had also learned that no matter how hopeless things might look, we must never give up. It was a valuable experience that we brought with us to Bamsebu. Yes, indeed, we are so vulnerable when things go wrong. Sudden challenges can seem hopeless and so scary, but to succeed in a moment like that is so freeing, bringing an indescribable peace. Suddenly, nothing is impossible.

Our Arctic overwintering at Bamsebu has illuminated the depths of who we are—our strengths, vulnerabilities, fears, loneliness, purpose, and all of the things we've learned through hardship. We have deep respect for this precious life we've been given and the beautiful land upon which we dwell. We don't need a dictionary to define commitment, camaraderie, love, perseverance, care, adaptation, and routine—we are living these words. Wilderness is the great teacher.

Imagine living in a medium-sized motor home, locked in with five other adults, for three years. That's what a mission to Mars would be like—an extreme situation, but at this point, we've all experienced some form of short-term lockdown. Living at Bamsebu for a year, we learned a lot about how energy goes where attention flows, and we want to share some insights on how short-term isolation can be an effective teacher—or at least, a powerful mirror of our daily choices and thoughts. We'd like to offer up some practices we adopted after living in a cabin for twelve months, as well as what we've learned from studying the early explorers.

During the pandemic, most people have been caught up in an over-whelm of Covid-19 news, Zoom calls, and so many new rules about how to live in this new world. A virus we can't see took over the world and almost robbed people of their joy and humour—not to mention the ability to travel. The pandemic has forced a hard stop on life as we know it.

"Expedition behavior" is a term used to describe the etiquette for interpersonal relationships and interactions, as laid out by mountaineer Paul Petzoldt at his National Outdoor Leadership School (NOLS). It means doing your fair share, remaining positive even when everything around you seems to be going wrong, extending kindness by, for instance, offering your expedition partner a warm drink and a smile after they've been outside chopping wood. It's teamwork, consideration, thoughtfulness, safety for all, and love—and it is without ego or rank.

We would like to encourage our readers to imagine that, during this Covid-19 crisis, we are all on a "global expedition" where specific behaviors and ways of being are vital to finding a healthy way forward. In this climate, each of us has an important role to play as an expedition member—our personal roles are more critical than ever. We all perform our roles as individuals, yet each behavior, action, and choice we make impacts the collective.

Overwintering in the Arctic through the polar night, stuck inside as storms raged outside, cold air whipping through the cracks in the walls, coming face-to-face with a polar bear, communication and equipment breakdowns—these defining moments made it easier for us to understand and adopt expedition behavior. We chose to self-isolate for the experience of living a dream adventure and for the sake of gathering data for science and learning about climate and biodiversity changes. We chose to stand up for what we believe in and to adopt a minimal lifestyle to highlight changes, to educate, and to reconnect with the natural world and ourselves.

None of you chose the isolation enforced by Covid-19. It chose you. Nonetheless, expedition behavior can help during challenging times by offering guidelines to forging a way forward together. Here are some characteristics of expedition behavior:

- Serve the mission and goals of the group.
- Be as concerned for others as you are for yourself.
- Treat everyone with dignity and respect.
- Support leadership and growth in everyone.
- Respect the cultures you contact.
- Be kind and openhearted.

- Do your share and stay organized.
- Model integrity by being honest and accountable.
- Admit and correct your mistakes.

Rank and status are irrelevant on an expedition—treating each other with respect and dignity means you leave your ego at the door before you walk in. This is especially important in the context of Covid-19, when so many people have lost their jobs and the identities that went along with them. After a blow like that, it's all too easy to feel a lack of worth—to feel that you don't count anymore and that no one sees you. But we have read numerous survival stories of early polar explorers who suffered great blows and emerged stronger.

Earlier, we wrote about how the Norwegian explorer Fridtjof Nansen was captivated by the northern lights. As a young scientist and outdoorsman, he was also determined to test the theory of polar drift. The far north was covered with ice, and the theory was that this ice cap had moved in a westerly direction across the Arctic. The genius of Nansen's plan was to build a ship for the expedition that was designed to rise up out of the ice as the floes pressed against her hull rather than resist the full force of the pressure. This ship was called the Fram, meaning "onward." So, the *Fram* headed into the Arctic pack ice where she was intentionally locked in, just north of 78º latitude—the same latitude as Bamsebu. Nansen's design worked according to plan, and the theory of polar drift was confirmed. When it appeared that the *Fram's* course would take her no further north across the polar ice cap, Nansen selected Hjalmar Johansen to accompany him on a dash to the pole with kayaks, sleds, and dogs.

They went as far as they could, navigating with dubious charts, but were caught by an early winter. They made it to Franz Josef Land, a Russian archipelago in the Arctic Ocean, and built a small hut out of stones and walrus hides in which they would live in complete isolation and confinement. The hut measured 2 x 3 meters (6 feet 7 inches x 9 feet 10 inches). Life was unpleasant, to say the least. For the entire nine-month Arctic winter, they cooked their food and illuminated their world with the small flame from a blubber lamp. The conditions were about as bad as humans can reasonably endure. When they slept, their dreams were filled with Turkish baths and visits to clothing stores.

How did this Norwegian polar expedition endure more than three years? The primary characteristic that distinguished Nansen from most other polar explorers was that he approached all aspects of expedition planning with scientific precision. He started by reading accounts of previous expeditions to learn from the experiences of his predecessors. Nansen remarked in his diary that most of the problems he faced had already been addressed and solved by previous explorers. He learned to wear appropriate clothing, pay special attention to food, select crew members who got along, and keep the crew busy and entertained. He fostered group solidarity through a respectful approach to his crew, treating everyone as an equal and ensuring that everyone had a voice, at a time when expeditions were typically run by one man calling the shots. More importantly, Nansen recognized that the physical and psychological well-being of his crew could make the difference between success and failure. Like explorer Roald Amundsen, who became the first person ever to reach the South Pole in 1911, he saw that, "The human factor is three quarters of any expedition."

The full account of Nansen and Johansen's Norwegian polar expedition is absolutely amazing and worth a thorough read (Farthest North, Fridtjof Nansen) They survived, but they suffered from the mind-numbing sameness of their days, among other health-threatening conditions. They emerged from their small den to perform all of the tasks necessary to fight their way through pack ice, back to the safety and comforts of civilization. Three years and three months after *Fram* first set sail, they were reunited with their crew and welcomed as if they had just returned from another planet.

None of us planned the "global expedition" we're now on—but we're on it, nonetheless. And since we find ourselves in this situation, we, like Nansen, can find comfort in discomfort. We can adopt expedition behavior and inhale fresh air, wonder, and curiosity, with a splash of love, care, and respect for each other and all things. In the isolation and confinement we're now experiencing, interpersonal problems are inevitable. Individual compatibility and recognizing the need for solidarity are among the key ingredients of any successful expedition, overwintering, or time of crisis.

We have had plenty of experience with nature since childhood and have taken on challenges well beyond our comfort zones over the years, but the intense and perilous forces we found in the Arctic and Antarctic were life-defining.

So, what inspires people to undertake great outdoor adventures? In recent decades, the number of people participating in adventure-oriented sports has seen an unprecedented increase. Some speculate that these "high-risk activities" are the bizarre contrivances of bored people who are a bit jaded with society, looking for a cheap thrill. This could be true, but we wonder if the trend speaks to a greater, more deeply rooted issue: Humans actually need adventure. We all need a healthy dose of challenge and adventure on a regular basis! Someone once said that if you're not living on the edge, you are taking up too much space.

We humans have lived ninety-nine times longer as hunters and gatherers than we have in the state called civilization. Not that long ago, we came to understand that the human body functions best when its daily life and routine include much more physical exercise than the average urban lifestyle has to offer. It has also been shown that just as the human body requires physical exercise to grow strong, the human spirit has a similar need for adventure.

Let's think of the hunters and gatherers who used to withstand storms, fight raging currents, and live their lives exposed to everything that the wilderness tossed their way. Back then, our ancestors thrived on peril and pursuit. Fear and stress were followed by exhilaration and relaxation.

Now that life has become so much tamer for so many of us, people are beginning to seek out the uncertain, the unrestrained, and the unpredictable in ever-greater numbers. This is a healthy striving, a striving after vibrancy and aliveness, critical not only to our individual health but also to our vitality and health as a species. We could all benefit from a daily dose of getting outside!

Our isolation deep in the high Arctic allowed for a deep connection to nature. We were answering the "call of the wild," or answering the call when "Mother Nature needs her daughters."

If the human race is going to avoid a catastrophe moving forward, we need to adopt a different set of values. Now is the perfect time to experiment with living differently, to become mindful users. There's no one-size-fits-all solution to climate change—the only way forward is for all humans to share resources, wisdom, and caring for each other, collectively and in community. The collective strength of all species lies in diversity, and we desperately need to collaborate to solve the world's most pernicious problems.

Polar bear at our doorstep.

Bamsebu after a storm battered us and Ettra on watch.

Fresh polar bear tracks.

Ptarmigan (they change color from summer to winter).

It's here! The first glimpse of the sun after three months of darkness!

Snowmobile trip during the midnight sun.

Measuring the Icecore—longest was 81 cm!

Christmas 2019 in our high heel shoes and dresses—doing it Arctic style.

Northern lights photographing in -21°C.

Pinkfooted geese.

Eggs from Pinkfooted geese.

February blue light and the full moon.

Chasing the light in the darkness.

Sunniva and Ettra at the ridge coming down from Berzelius fjellet.

Young polar bears on sea ice just outside Bamsebu—they were very curious!

Safe drone landing. Ettra, Hilde, and Sunniva, Sea ice on VanKeulenfjorden.

Modern day replica of old school Aurora photographers.

Celebrating May 17th, which is Norway's National Day.

Good morning! Our neighbor just outside our door.

Svalbard Reindeer—facing west to Stuptinden and Aclive kammen.

Staying in shape with a run on the seaice; we used the snowmobile to ride onto the ice for wide open views as it was easier to spot polar bears.

All in a days work—standing with our icecore findings.

Celebrating our citizen science work and the National Day of Norway.

CHAPTER 8

THE POLAR NIGHT

When the night has come
And the land is dark
And the moon is the only light we'll see,
No, I won't be afraid
Oh, I won't be afraid,
Just as long as you stand, stand by me.
— Ben E. King

The first time we tried to walk in total darkness was in September 2018. We were on a five-day hike together on the historic Italian pilgrim trail Via Francigena. One of the guides had been blind since birth, and her senses were so keen that our curiosity was piqued. How in the world could she walk on the narrow trails with no sight and not end up in the ditch? We accepted her challenge, closed our eyes, and walked. Our timed, two-minute walk with our eyes closed yielded much insight as we listened for her footsteps and followed her, step by step. We felt so vulnerable without vision. Rocks and leaves beneath our feet. The wind, its sound. The chatter of conversation behind us, in front of us. Our breath, thoughts, insecurities, and our heartbeats. Guilia was the guide's name. She had much to teach, and we had much to learn.

At Bamsebu, we were in total darkness. Eyes wide open with nothing to see. Dark. Dark, save for the random, fast-moving satellites, shootings stars, and those many magical auroral displays that felt like they were shining just for us. When it was overcast and there was no moonlight, it was too dark to see any land features or even a single step in front of us, so we would use our headlamps, the strongest of which shone at 12,000 lumens. We also had one pair of night vision binoculars. We would scan the area, 360 degrees, before heading out for a short walk in this long polar night. We would look for the glow of distant eyes. When we saw two eyes shining, they would paralyze us with fear but also with a strange and curious sense of wonder. *Is that a reindeer or a polar bear?* It was hard to reason with the voices in our heads—insecurity can easily breed fear, making the power of those voices hard to fight. If you think you see a polar bear, you become almost convinced it must be one since you can't prove otherwise.

Stepping outside into the polar night also involved an expedition into getting dressed. Base layers, down pants, down jacket, outer layer of pants, and a bulky jacket that inflated you two sizes. Neck gaiter, hat, headlamp, insulated boots, gloves (usually two pairs), and, finally, a big, hefty belt with our flare gun, revolver, knife, and a Swiss tool. It was warmer inside, so the goal was always to get dressed and head outside quickly.

We would always go together. First, we would crack open the wooden door to our entryway, where our power bank sat. Then we'd open the wooden door to the outside and scan both sides of Bamsebu before venturing further. Even if we tricked ourselves into believing there was nothing out there because we couldn't hear anything, when we opened the door onto the darkness, we were instantly reminded that you're never alone in the dark polar night. Case in point: Twice there was a polar bear just meters from the front door when we opened it. There are five to six bears that are known to frequent our area, and the largest one weighs over 600 kg (1,323 lbs)—and that, my friends, is almost about the same size as Bamsebu! Well, it feels like it, anyway.

With each side of the hut cleared and no visible polar bear tracks in the snow, we would step further out onto the frozen tundra, scanning for moving objects, animal prints in the snow, and the glow of distant eyes. We moved deliberately, with caution and patience, starting our slow plod past Skarpsyn and up to the rock marker—a cairn that sits at the top of a small ridge south of Bamsebu. The terrain was uneven, it was dark, and the blowing snow would reduce visibility. We would trip, we lose our balance, and regain it. There would be no rhythm to our walking.

SUNNIVA

On one particular day, I wasn't feeling good about our outing, but we kept marching. It was dark, snow was blowing sideways, and I could barely see my feet. We stopped just below the cairn on the hill, and I told Hilde that I was nervous. I couldn't see a thing, and I was convinced there was something out there. Then, suddenly, I became sure I had lost the satellite phone: "SHIT!" I shouted. "The phone's gone! I had it right here in my pocket. What are we going to do? I have to go back!" All of this spoken in an elevated tone—I was so irritated at myself.

Hilde replied in a calm-ish voice, at least a few decibels below mine, "Are you sure it was in that pocket?"

"YES, I am SURE!"

Her headlamp scanned the pocket I was sure it had fallen out of—then another pocket right next to it. There was the darn antenna, sticking out of the exact pocket I had stuck it in.

"There it is," she said with a smile. I tried to smile back, but I was too embarrassed. The snowmobile suit I was wearing had about six pockets on each side, and to be honest, they were hard to keep track of. And with gloves on, I would fumble—I'd try to be precise in my actions, but I just couldn't. Everything was bulky and made me feel clumsy, like a tiny person walking in a giant's boots and clothes. Just the thought of being back at Bamsebu, stripped down to long johns and a familiar version of myself, was sometimes enough to make me head for the "barn."

The dark is a strange thing, and the thoughts that show up in it can be hard to understand. The anxiety, the insecurity, the things you're sure you see and feel: They're all real to you. This is the inherent struggle, especially when you live so far from anyone else and any external stimulation. The experience seems similar to people's descriptions of fighting depression and loneliness. And indeed, we had our own internal struggles with our emotions in that tiny space. Small seeds of irritation would get planted without our conscious knowing, then another day would arrive, and mysteriously that same irritation would get triggered, the seed would get watered, and it would grow. It was a slow and slippery slope, this kind of irritation—and one that's long been studied for insights on coping with stress in astronauts and those living in isolated quarters such as remote camps in Antarctica and the Arctic.

One such story unfolds in Antarctica, where two men were alone at a base for what was to be longer than either wanted. They had chores and maintenance to keep up with and cooking to do—there was plenty to keep them busy. In their time off, both men liked to read, and just like us at Bamsebu, what they brought was what they had, so their selection was limited. They ended up reading the same books over and over. One guy—let's call him Alex—started to irritate the other—let's call him Juan—by spoiling the endings of books before Juan had a chance to finish them. The first time this happened, Juan apparently waved his fist in the air at Alex. Darn him for spoiling the adventure he was on with his book! But then it happened twice more—enough to provoke such resentment and anger in Juan that he shot Alex. They did get rescued, and their base mission was cut short—but deviant behavior had prevailed! Can you imagine? Ohhh, I would have socked him too, but not with a bullet.

Feeling powerless over another and powerless even over your own irritation—it makes you want to take back your power, however irrationally that might happen.

Hilde and I are peaceful women, neither one of us inclined toward anger or bursts of any form of violence. We are so thankful for this because if it weren't the case, we could have encountered a number of worst-case scenarios. We had to trust each other with our lives— literally. That trust was at the very root of what made our thriving possible. With this trust, we developed a bond that was unshakeable.

One of the kids on our monthly satellite call asked, "Why it is so dark there right now?" Given our location relative to the sun and the fact that the earth tilts at 23.5°, at 78°, we were too far north for the sun to reach us. We were in total darkness from November 14 to January 19—not even a hint of the sun.

When it's dark, most of us go into some form of human hibernation. When the shorter days of winter arrive, we often cocoon ourselves: It's almost like a yearly invitation to renew, sleep, and be quiet—a time for regeneration of the body, mind, and your senses, and to miss a gym workout. Or two. Or four. The dark gives us permission to relax more. For those of you reading this on the couch with your favorite bag of potato chips—we see you, and we're right there with you. We, too, took more time to fill our tanks at Bamsebu: to read, write, take care of our many daily chores, and also to refill by going outside at every opportunity, photographing the northern lights for NASA, flying the drone for BCIT when the winds were calm, and observing wildlife.

Few people live in the dark 24/7. Even our artificial light inside wasn't as bright as we were used to; it was more of a soft, yellow light. Very cozy, but it never made us feel fully awake. Living in the dark makes you sleepy, throws off your body rhythms, amplifies all of the otherwise tempered voices in your head, and plays with your emotions. So, we both took our daily doses of Vitamin D and stayed active.

Even so, depression can be very real in the polar night. In the Nordic countries, many have taken their own lives as an internal emptiness grows to mirror the external darkness. Thankfully, neither of us got depressed, and we packed many tools to help us handle the small space we were in, the mental challenges we would go through, and the fact of living on top of each other. The darkness brought up so many hidden sides of our personalities, but we had brought tools to manage those, too, since we were far from any help we might need.

During the polar night, our world was a contrast of black night and white snow. The sounds of the howling and whistling wind were loud enough to keep us awake at night, listening for any tiny, unfamiliar sound of something lurking in the dark and ravaging one of our food barrels. Anything could happen, so we had to be prepared. Some nights we'd take shifts shoveling the snow that could pile up outside of the door—two-hour shifts of shoveling to make it possible to safely open the door. Being trapped inside wasn't an option since it brought its own darkness.

In 1934, painter Christiane Ritter left her home in Austria for Spitsbergen to spend a year there with her husband. Her book about the experience, *A Woman in the Polar Night*, is a classic. It's such a powerful read that we had to share some passages here:

> *The days go by uneventfully, without any real work, without a consoling glimpse into the reality of the world. At night we lie down, neither tired nor wakeful, encompassed by the unending darkness and the profound quiet.*

Surrounded by this boundless deadness and rigidity of everything physical, one's living senses begin slowly to go their own way. More frequently and more brightly as the winter is prolonged, a strange light spreads before the inner eye, a remote and yet familiar vision. It is as though here, in this apartness, we develop a particularly sharp awareness of the mighty laws of the spirit, of the unfathomable gulf between human magnitudes and eternal truth. Outside of time, everything is annihilated. The imprisoned senses circle in the past, in a scene without spatial dimensions, a play in which time stands still.

What's it like to be unable to see where you're going, to not see your destination? How much do you trust yourself? Are you equipped to handle the surprises along the way? When you feel scared or confronted, will fear take over?

At Bamsebu, we found ourselves in a most natural state. We felt privileged to share this unique part of our world and to experience nature's constant miracles, minute by minute, day after day. The total darkness, a sky full of stars, the shifting ice, the auroral displays, the moon—and then, an Arctic that began to slowly wake up from its sleep. Little by little, then with increasing speed, soft light appeared, followed by the magic pastel light of Svalbard. By April, we had the midnight sun: twenty-four hours of daylight.

To bear witness to this entire cycle is nothing short of unbelievable. It has been said that Antarctica, with its sheet of vast white, is "no more than a mirror, to reflect back and make large what we truly are," and perhaps the same could be said for the polar night: yet another mirror to reflect back and make large what we truly are.

CHAPTER 9

DANGER + OPPORTUNITY

THE CLIMATE CRISIS AND COVID-19

What lies behind us and what lies before us are tiny
matters compared to what lies within us.
— Ralph Waldo Emerson

What if the isolation imposed by Covid-19 gave us all a small chance to come out stronger, more connected and loving to each other, more informed, kinder, and with greater awareness of our habits and how we engage day-to-day?

Who would have thought when we started *Hearts in the Ice* that we would find ourselves sitting at Bamsebu receiving news that the entire world had become completely unhinged by a coronavirus? *Corona?* Corona was a cold beer and the town Sunniva's sister lived in. Now, of course, coronavirus and Covid-19 are household names.

The first rumblings we heard about a virus were that it had spread through Italy and eventually forced the country into lockdown. The news came in short texts via Facebook Messenger—the way we typically received information from Maria Philippa Rossi, who was handling our social media outreach. It was impossible to understand what it all meant or to get a full picture of what the Italians and the rest of Europe were dealing with at that point. That was March 8. Soon after, we heard vague notions that this virus seemed to strike the elderly in particular. Then there was specific talk of a "pandemic" that had already flourished around the eastern half of the world, with its origins in China. What the heck was going on?

As you know, we had no TV or radio, no switch we could flick to get the news in real time. It was completely surreal to have no news or pictures, just the odd Messenger notifications, short emails, and bits and pieces of information about what was going on out there. We felt powerless. The world was experiencing a global pandemic while we were away at Bamsebu.

Then came the first small bit of news that impacted us directly. The videographer for our documentary had to cancel a trip to Bamsebu to finish some filming—he had an autoimmune disease and was in the vulnerable category for the virus and advised not to travel.

Just a few days later, while we were tucked inside with a storm raging outside, an even bigger storm, unlike anything the world had seen, was intensifying. We were starting to feel the emotions and the fear. Whole regions and even entire countries went into lockdown. More and more people went into quarantine—a word most people had rarely even heard but which had now become a binding rule for many. At this point, we had been in self-imposed "quarantine" for seven months. We couldn't possibly imagine people quarantining in cities.

On March 12, the governor of Svalbard ordered an inspection to evaluate the adaptations we had made to the exterior of the cabin since Bamsebu is a cultural heritage site in addition to being a private cabin. They came to check out the solar panel, the windmill, and the sheets of black paper stapled to the east wall for wind protection. The three inspectors arrived by helicopter, visiting on behalf of the Norwegian Directorate for Cultural Heritage.

There was a cold wind blowing outside, and the inspectors wanted to come inside. But we hadn't had visitors in the cabin since the year before and were feeling vulnerable with all the news of the pandemic. We hadn't had a single cold or sore throat—we felt healthier than ever before. And now, all of a sudden, visitors wanted to come inside the cabin?

With so little news, and with the news we did get focusing on the climbing death toll, we had a lot of questions about Covid-19. How did it spread? What did a "total lockdown" mean? Who decided that one meter or six feet was a good distance? Where did it start? And most pressingly: Was it really a good idea to invite them in? Well, they were invited in.

The day after our visit from the three inspectors, the school, nursery school, and gym in Longyearbyen were closed down, and the entire town went into lockdown.

Without radio, TV, or regular internet, we weren't exposed to the same sensory input that was bombarding the rest of the world on a daily basis: the number of people infected and the death toll increasing every minute. Fear and unrest, social distancing, empty streets and shops, a world that had come to a halt. Uncertainty about the future, with threats to health, security, and the economy on the personal, national, and international levels. Though we weren't experiencing these things directly from our isolated little spot at Bamsebu, we started to feel others' isolation, worry, fear, sadness, loss, uncertainty, and upheaval.

Spring equinox in 2020 gave new meaning to the words "March madness." It was unfathomable, what was really happening out there, the depths of despair and devastation people had sunk to, and the volume of change everyone was navigating. Plan A had become plan B, C, D, and so on. Change was the only constant.

March 17, 2020, was Sunniva's birthday—a day we would normally have celebrated, but instead, with heavy hearts, we delivered the news to our family, friends, partners, sponsors, and special guests that we would be cancelling our May pickup expedition. The May pickup trip was to be our grand finale and a celebration of our historic, successful winter stay, complete with everyone who had helped build the foundation for *Hearts in the Ice*. Some of the guests who were planning to attend had been on our send-off trip and would have returned to exactly the same place where they had dropped us off the previous September—we hadn't moved or even had a shower since they saw us last.

We had so been looking forward to this event and had worked all winter to plan it, down to the smallest details, spending a fortune on satellite data transfers for all the correspondence and passing many hours of the dark polar night planning logistics and details. It had been our light in the darkness. But it was not to be. Cancelling was the only right thing to do—everyone's safety was paramount. The world had been upended, and we, too, needed to adjust our bearings. The energy inside the cabin was heavy with uncertainty.

Still, life at Bamsebu went on as usual, with challenges small and large, foreseen and unforeseen. The sun returned, and with it, active wildlife and beautiful light conditions. Nature kept delivering small miracles. And, too, Mother Earth and civilization alike were experiencing less human activity and cleaner air. Things were getting quieter. Everything was taking a breather without us. It felt like a new version of Rachel Carson's *Silent Spring*, where she describes a spring without birdsong—but this time, it was the people who were quiet and the birds who were singing. All trips had been cancelled and plans thwarted, and the energy had been turned toward a rescue mission for humankind and our planet.

At the same time as news of the pandemic began to trickle in, so too did media requests—people wanting interviews about how we coped in isolation. Did we have any tips? Soon, we were receiving a flood of interest from media around the world. We were considered experts in isolation, and people wanted to hear our thoughts about how we had managed to make it through all these months. This became an enormous undertaking, and we were once again grateful that we had Maria and Pascale Lortie, who handled all sponsors and media for us, to manage and filter all of the requests. Most requests came in via email, but we also conducted numerous telephone interviews.

Even with all this going on, we wanted to keep serving and supporting our world's diminishing natural spaces, loss of species, and highlighting the impacts of not taking care of this planet. And increasingly, we saw reason to hope: As countries took ever bolder steps to curb the rate of infection and deaths, we saw that an entire world could adapt if it had to—and if it had functioning, effective leadership.

For *Hearts in the Ice*, we had to decide. What should we do? Where were we most relevant? What could we do with the powerful platform and community we had created? We also had to rethink our personal plans: We had both made lots of arrangements for the summer that included, among other things, meeting up with all of our near and dear loved ones. But like everyone else, we had to think in new ways. As for work: We were both in the expedition-cruise industry back home in our regular lives, and there was little movement in the industry at that time. No one was actively planning trips for the near future, so there was little contribution we could make there.

In the end, we decided to stay beyond our nine months at Bamsebu. Our research partners wanted us to keep collecting the data we had been gathering for the past nine months since there was no one out in the field due to Covid-19 and no help from expedition-cruise tourists, either. Typically, these tourists voluntarily collect plastic on the beaches and help collect data throughout the summer season with their onboard "Citizen Science" programs.

First, we took a week away from Bamsebu. Covid-19 had not yet been detected in Longyearbyen and wouldn't be through the entire Arctic summer. So, in early May, we departed for Longyearbyen via snowmobile, with sleds in tow. It was a massive operation to get back to civilization for the first time in nine months and a wonderful trip—great snow conditions and excellent visibility. We took all of our empty containers, water jugs, gear, and so on. Our most precious resource, Ettra, was tucked inside her crate on the sled behind the snowmobile—though she liked it best when we let her out of the crate and she could run beside us with her head held high and proud, racing across the frozen tundra, completely free. Both of us stole many glances at her in her element.

The week in town was crazy and so jam-packed with activities, feelings, jarring transitions, and culture shock that it would have knocked the air out of most people. We recorded an interview with Hazel Pfeifer from CNN for a program called Call to Earth that would air in December 2020. Besides this, there were more TV interviews, online meetings and gatherings, stores and cafes to visit, and access to showers. The transition was overwhelming. And amid it all, there was a deep sadness. Things were so uncertain. The world was so different from the one we had left.

After a week in Longyearbyen, we headed back to Bamsebu on our snowmobiles with Ettra and some equipment in tow. That summer, all citizen research activity was on hold. We were the only citizen scientists collecting data for our research partners—and also among the rare few people out and about picking up plastic debris, fishing nets (which reindeer antlers often get caught in), and other forms of garbage that had washed up on shore. It was completely surreal that the world outside of Bamsebu had come to a screeching halt.

Normally, there would have been plenty of expedition-cruise tourists doing this work with us. The industry had been engaged in clean-up efforts in Svalbard for the last twenty years with "Clean up Svalbard" and also a new worldwide program called Clean Seas established in 2017.

The program was initiated by the United Nations Environment Programme (UNEP) with the purpose of engaging governments, private businesses, and the general public in the fight against marine plastic pollution.

The Clean Seas project suffered tragedy on Sunday, March 10, 2019, when Sarah Auffret, environmental agent at the Association of Arctic Expedition Cruise Operators (AECO), was killed. She was on her way to Nairobi to talk about the Clean Seas project in connection with the UN Environment Assembly when her Ethiopian Airlines flight crashed soon after take-off from Addis Ababa, with no survivors. Sarah touched the lives of hundreds of people and inspired the people around her to make a difference. And her legacy lives on: Every June 16 since her death, people around the world have conducted clean-ups in their local environments, a global effort to mark Sarah's birthday. We both knew Sarah very well.

Thanks to Clean Seas and other efforts, for many visitors, a trip to the Arctic becomes a chance to reflect on some of the most pressing environmental challenges of our time. It can be a formative experience when they set foot on the beaches that they had expected to be pristine, only to find them at times littered with marine debris. Waste from everywhere in the world can end up in the Arctic, transported by ocean currents, and marine litter puts Arctic wildlife at risk—as we learned from NPI researcher Geir Gabrielsen. He shared that nine out of ten fulmars found dead that day had ingested plastic and then, inevitably, died of starvation. Fulmars mistake plastic for a food source, and this, in turn, renders their stomachs incapable of processing any food at all—a truly sad and unnecessary fate. In a true collaborative effort, AECO encourages all members to join its mission to achieve safe, responsible, environmentally friendly tourism in the Arctic. These operators and their guests have helped to clean up Svalbard. In recent years, about twenty tons of waste have been removed from beaches in Svalbard every summer.

But there's always more trash.

In fact, today, the Arctic is dealing with new sources of pollution and debris related to Covid-19 in the form of masks, gloves, hand sanitizer bottles, and single-use gowns.

Staying on at Bamsebu gave us the chance to keep boosting knowledge backed by experts, as we had done throughout the winter—and now, we could give our partners and sponsors even more content and support.

We had chosen to stay, but what did that mean? What would we need? And how would we do all this extra work while also supplementing our provisions and taking care of our mental health?

When we arrived back at the hut, everything seemed to have changed. In a way, we had finished one thing and were about to start another, which felt new. The transition felt jarring, and not just because of the changes in us, but because of those all around us at Bamsebu. Spring had come more quickly than we had expected, and the resupply we had expected from Longyearbyen on May 17 couldn't make it to us because of the ice conditions. The snow and ice were disappearing, and with them, the option of going out on the snowmobile came to an abrupt halt. Skiing conditions were lousy. Then the ice completely disappeared. The tundra was wet and delicate, and we felt stuck. We had nowhere to go. We couldn't walk on the soggy, fragile tundra since our feet would leave a lasting imprint; skiing and snowmobiling were over; kayak weather wasn't here yet; and there were no ships around. We were isolated in every possible way.

Meanwhile, everything was in transition. With the spring came the geese in all their glory—and by the hundreds. They had flown a long way, and they came to rest on the bare earth and feed eagerly on the rich vegetation. All the migratory birds arrived in a short window, and the reindeer had company on the tundra around Bamsebu. Together with Ettra, we followed all their movements, watching how some settled and built nests while others flew further north on the island. And even before all the snow was gone, the beautiful, colorful mountain flowers started to peek out. Gorgeous. Despite our isolation, we felt so fortunate to be able to continue with our data collection, education outreach, and communication with the outside world. This gave us purpose. Undoubtedly, we had something to contribute from here. Our decision to stay for the summer—nearly four more months—felt so right and relevant.

Some changes are subtle, like clouds brewing into a storm or the seasons changing. Others are strong, clear indicators of a changing climate and the adaptations it forces—like the polar bear hunting and killing a reindeer instead of a seal, its usual food source. We observed this two times, and according to the experts, it is a possible sign of polar bear behavior adapting to the lack of seals on the ice.

The very kernel of Hearts is the Ice is our attempt to bring the world together around a climate and natural crisis we've known about for decades, but perhaps didn't quite grasp, or whose severity we didn't fully understand. The alarm bells went off long ago around climate change and its impact on humans, other species, and economics. There is a way forward, and it involves all humans sharing our resources, wisdom, and caring for each other, collectively and in community. Change never happens overnight, but it does always start with us.

The last few years have been tough. We know how challenging it is to be isolated with only one person 24/7. It takes a ton of painful self-awareness and buckets of patience, kindness, and love to make the best of a tough situation, day after day. Are you looking around at this Covid-19 crisis and feeling helpless because you have limited power to stop it? That's how many of us have long been feeling about the climate crisis for many years. But there is hope for us stubborn optimists.

The way the world was able to mobilize and shut down in the blink of an eye to properly respond to the Covid-19 crisis is proof that political leaders actually do have the ability to make rapid change—when they want to.

So where is that rapid response for the climate crisis?

Whether we like it or not, and whether we choose to accept the science or not, the reality of climate change is upon us. It's affecting everything—not just weather patterns, ecozystems, ice sheets, coastlines, and cities across the planet, but also the health, safety, and security of every person alive and the generations to come. Scientists have warned that we have less than a decade to completely transform the way our entire economy and world runs and that we need to transition to renewable energy and sustainable agriculture in order to slow the rapid escalation of climate change. Yet, we continue to plough ahead with business as usual, paving the way for a future of extreme weather events, mass displacement, disease, famine, and death. That's not hyperbole; these are the predictions and findings of experts who have devoted their careers to this issue.

What would it look like if the world actually decided to take on the climate crisis? It would look similar to what we have seen during the pandemic: 24/7 media coverage of the issue, consistent headlines reporting updated death tolls, experts appearing on the news daily to update the public on the crisis, and everyone stopping everything and putting the world on pause to deal with the immediate crisis at hand. The coronavirus response is showing us how people can mobilize and do their part when it's properly communicated to them that we are indeed in an urgent crisis. The parallels are not exact, and the world's Covid-19 response is not a perfect template for the mobilization that's necessary for climate justice. For one thing, the pandemic response is simply trying to mitigate a disaster, while an urgent climate response would not only mitigate disaster but actively create a better world.

And yet the past years have shown us that this kind of change is possible.

So, where do we go from here? That's the big question. Once the pandemic is under control, the world cannot exhale and go back to normal. We need to move on to tackling the other deadly crisis that cannot wait.

CHAPTER 10

A COMMUNITY OF BADASS WOMEN

WHY WE NEED FEMALE LEADERS

Our deepest fear is not that we are inadequate. Our deepest fear is that we are powerful beyond measure. It is our light, not our darkness, that most frightens us. We ask ourselves, 'Who am I to be brilliant, gorgeous, talented, fabulous?' Actually, who are you not to be? . . . And as we let our own light shine, we unconsciously give other people permission to do the same. As we are liberated from our own fear, our presence automatically liberates others.
— Marianne Williamson

*H*ow in the world can two women survive and thrive while overwintering alone together in the Arctic?

This is a question many might want to ask, and they might bring many stereotypes into the conversation with them. We have to wonder whether the same questions and the same curiosities would arise if two men had overwintered together. Most likely not: To be a trapper and to overwinter through a full winter, including the three-plus months of a long polar night, has traditionally been a male endeavor. We women still have to defy stereotypes, and perhaps more importantly, stand up and stand together.

Typically, when men engage in something death-defying, brands seem to clamour to offer them sponsorship opportunities. It was tough for us to get funding from sponsors for our project, at least initially. As women, we have had to fight harder, but slowly we are changing the rules as two capable women, working hard to promote collaboration rather than competition.

Hilde remembers the first time she heard there was a female pilot flying her plane, and Sunniva remembers the first female CEO she met—both professions that have traditionally been dominated by men. There are badass women everywhere! We are pilots, governors of Svalbard, prime ministers, CEOs, presidents, adventurers, mothers, sisters, aunts, and daughters.

So back to the question: *How in the world can two women survive and thrive while overwintering alone together in the Arctic?*

Answer: We survived and thrived because we are both women. We handled our overwintering just fine, with strength, courage, grace, and ability. We cared for each other, communicated, shared the load, and were equals who trusted and respected each other.

We had our health and our individual and collective strength. As women, we also excel at building relationships: We had a strong foundation of family, friends, and supporters; a formidable network of sponsors and research partners; and each other. It was really the powerful collaborative community we had amassed that made our work global in scale and interest. We also learned to ask for help—another skill at which women often excel. Here are some words of wisdom from people in our network:

WHY FEMALE LEADERSHIP IS SO IMPORTANT

B ecause the world is in turmoil on so many levels—and so much of male leadership is based on the race for economic gain, not on human and animal interactions and the symbiotic relationship we should have with this earth—females seem more inclined to see and work toward this more important picture.

— ESTHER GRANT

T he best way I can say this is that women embody two of the four principles of creation itself, and without all four principles in action, there is no moving forward. These four principles of creation are woven into the universal principles of the masculine and feminine—the principles are love and wisdom, strength and intelligence. The feminine is "in charge of," or we could say is the embodiment of, love and wisdom, and the masculine is in charge of strength and intelligence.

Strength and intelligence are the capacities we have for expressing love and wisdom, for putting love and wisdom to life-positive work in the world. We live in a culture that has denied the importance of the feminine, and without this, we end up just wielding power that has no love. Intelligence is just the capacity to express wisdom; it is not the wisdom itself. By itself, not connected to wisdom, intelligence does nothing.

Imagine bringing strength to love again and intelligence to wisdom again. We can only do this when we bring the feminine together again with the masculine—in this properly woven state, the feminine leads. It is our natural way of being. This is how full consciousness works.

We need to understand that these principles are never separate—we can convince ourselves that they are cut apart, we can attempt to suppress them, but they are always working toward union and expression. When human action denies this dynamic, we are the ones who break what the underlying natural system produces.

— MARTI SPIEGELMAN, LEADERSHIP ADVISOR, MENTOR, SPEAKER, FOUNDER, SHAMAN'S LIGHT (INDIGENOUS INITIATION AND MENTORING PROGRAM)

*A*s with everything in life, balance is so very important . . . in order for that to happen we need representation from all directions, including the female voice and perspective.

— CAROLYN STROUD

*T*he world needs the best from all the talents of the world in these challenging times. Many young talents are lost because of lack of opportunity, stimulation, faith in their own ability, and so many other unfortunate circumstances. Society is losing/wasting many talents among the young, and in particular among girls. Educating girls and young women (particularly in the less affluent countries, but also among underprivileged groups in affluent countries) is the most important thing we can do to create a better future for humankind and the world. I hope Hearts in the Ice can inspire and salvage some talents by conveying a message about believing

in yourself. May as many as possible fulfillll themselves, with permission to pursue their dreams and the tools to shape their own futures.
— KIM HOLMÉN, INTERNATIONAL DIRECTOR,
NORWEGIAN POLAR INSTITUTE

*T*hey *are realiztic; they hope for the best and plan for the worst.*
Relationships are more important to them than power.
This is what every human needs to feel: the leadership of inclusion and feeling held.
A leadership that serves you instead of overpowering you.
Women think more holistically.
Heart signals affect the pain center in the brain, which is involved in decision-making, creativity, and emotional experience.
Look at true leadership in a crisis. Look at Covid-19.
Women are stepping up to show the world how to manage our human family. In Iceland, Taiwan, Germany, New Zealand, Finland, and Denmark, this pandemic is revealing that women have what it takes when the heat rises.
These female leaders have communicated a different message than we are used to. It was like their arms held you close in a heartfelt and loving embrace.
Who knew leaders could sound like this?
— CARINA VINBERG, LEADERSHIP AND PERSONAL COACH

*B*ecause *we must inspire youth so they can have confidence in becoming leaders too, without restrictions.*
— ANA ROSA MARISCAL, CORPORATE COMMUNICATIONS, BRP

*I*t's *important for leaders to lead with kindness and compassion, regard-less of their gender. The reason we find it particularly inspiring in this day when a woman leads is because women have often taken the back seat to a man in adventures like this one. So, it still feels quite new. But if we really look closely at reality and not just how we feel about reality, women have been leading for millennia. Only now have the men started noticing.*
— JOSS STONE, SINGER, SONGWRITER

*W*hether it's by conditioning or "bred in the bone," ample research shows us that women are more collaborative, inclusive, legacy-minded, and trusted with assets (money and people). Evidence suggests that as leaders, they have the competencies that make for very good leadership, statistically significantly more than men in many instances. At a time when the practice of leadership is under scrutiny, when overwhelmingly people don't trust leadership—feel that they are short-sighted, self-interested, not committed to protecting the planet for the greater good, rather than people who can change the approach, can help all of us create the future we want—it seems self-evident that we would encourage women to step up in significant numbers.

— FABIAN DATTNER, LEADERSHIP EXPERT, FOUNDER, HOMEWARD BOUND PROJECTS

I believe female entrepreneurship and the presence of women in management teams have a positive influence on the social motivations and achievements of teams and organizations.

Female leadership matters. Studies have shown that companies with greater diversity are more profitable.

I strongly believe female leadership and diversity, in general, will lead to better working environments and better understanding—bringing different perspectives to the table. As a woman and parent, I'm passionate about ensuring that the next generation does not inherit outdated ideas of women's and men's roles and characteristics. We have the opportunity to radically shift old-fashioned characteristics of men and women and evolve a more balanced, diverse, and ultimately more flexible and resilient way of doing business.

— CAROLINE GRØNVOLD, VP PRODUCT & INNOVATION, HURTIGRUTEN

WHY COLLABORATION IS KEY

*S*trength in numbers is always going to be more powerful. It's statistically and mathematically a no-brainer.

— ESTHER GRANT

H *earts in the Ice kind of reminds me of the first moonwalk. Once people have done it, it increases interest and the possibility of others doing it too. It makes it more real. The collaboration of scientists with "citizen scientists" is such a powerful collaboration.*
— ANNABELLE JANE MURRAY, ARTIST

E *veryone should collaborate—we are not designed to go solo. We are collective beings. Where women are concerned, creation never occurs by bringing one thing together with itself. Creation occurs when two things come together and ignite the creation of a third thing. Women are the primary stewards of this process. Creation itself is a collaborative process, and the stewardship of what is created requires collaboration. As the masters of creation, women must collaborate so they can ignite their deeper collective value and central role in the well-being of all life. In the Andean traditions, they say that in the first half of life, women create life itself, and in the second half of life, women create wisdom. None of this can be achieved solo. When women collaborate, they can spark the collective memory of the wisdom and love that is required for our well-being on a global scale.*
— MARTI SPIEGELMAN, LEADERSHIP ADVISOR, MENTOR, SPEAKER, FOUNDER, SHAMAN'S LIGHT (INDIGENOUS INITIATION AND MENTORING PROGRAM)

W *e need all voices represented, which also benefits and empowers us all.*
— CAROLYN STROUD

W *hen we collaborate and feel trust in a trusting environment, we go from I-centered to WE-centered and are not addicted to being right, not protective or sceptical, not using power to convince. Listening is the key. We have open minds—we are not only saying that we have open minds; we have them biologically; we can use our entire brains: the prefrontal cortex, the neocortex, and all the parts that sing along very well if TRUST is what we want to build. We can avoid creating the "fight, flight, or freeze" mode.*
— CARINA VINBERG, LEADERSHIP AND PERSONAL COACH

I think everyone should collaborate; it's very nice to see women collaborating because women are known for being competitive with each other where there is no competition to be had. That's nature at work. I love to see women coming together with unity and love for each other. It shouldn't be rare, but I have noticed that it can be. So, we have a bit of a responsibility to do as much as possible so the drama can disappear, and we can collaborate in harmony.

— JOSS STONE, SINGER, SONGWRITER

C itizen-science projects ARE the future. Whether it's through funding, supporting a project(s), or contributing through your own effort, this is how change will happen.

The enormity of the problem we face with climate change can be overwhelming to the point of despair and paralyzis. The great scientist and environmentalist Jane Goodall spoke to this issue once, and her words have not only rung true for us, but they are words we now work hard to live by. When asked how it was that she was able to stay positive and have hope in a world of such dire climate calamity and environmental destruction, she said, "Save what you can touch."

For us, citizen-science projects are the embodiment of this simple philosophy, and in this way, their potential knows no bounds.

— KATHLEEN URDAHL AND SHENA HINKS

I 'm not sure I need to give advice on this. It is what we naturally predispose to do. More importantly, I would say women need to know that it is probably the most important attribute of leadership (for men and women) right now. We desperately need to collaborate to solve some of the world's most pernicious problems.

— FABIAN DATTNER, LEADERSHIP EXPERT, FOUNDER,
HOMEWARD BOUND PROJECTS

C ollaboration is key to educating and engaging the next generations of students. Trafalgar School for Girls is thrilled to have been able to attend the monthly calls through Exploring by the Seat of Your Pants and to have had a special direct call, which brought in some of Sunniva's former teachers as well as other old girls who currently work in the field of climate change. Connecting experts in related fields within the Traf alumnae network alone is a great start.

Hearts in the Ice and Trafalgar School are currently collaborating on a philanthropic proposal that will see the funding of a climate-care forum/climate-care ambassador program at Trafalgar. Providing funds for the professional development of teachers to learn how to best integrate climate-care themes across the curriculum, bringing in experts on the topic to address students, giving students hands-on projects, and transforming them into citizen scientists are just a few of the ideas for this. This model could be repeated at schools all over the world. After all, students will be key to the future of humanity.

— SHARON COZENS, DIRECTOR OF
ADVANCEMENT, SELWYN HOUSE SCHOOL

I hope projects like Hearts in the Ice inspire individuals to see that vision, drive, a good idea, and passion can bring people together for a great cause. HITI has shown us that one idea can unite people across cultures, language, geography, age, art, music, and science, and that kind of work is needed in the world. So many complex problems to solve in the world, and projects like this show us that good ideas can come from anywhere.

Addressing climate change and solving some of its most intractable challenges will require us to bring people together from different backgrounds and perspectives so that new ideas and collaboration can emerge. It was a meaningful reminder that in my role as leader, my job is not to come up with all of the solutions but to focus on creating the space and time for people to come together.

— KAREN ELLIOTT, MAYOR, SQUAMISH,
BRITISH COLUMBIA, CANADA

W hen we collaborate or brainstorm with the right team, we can evoke new, unique ideas and increase productivity.

Collaborating allows individuals to share their experiences along with the mistakes they made along the way. It cuts back on the blunders and bad decisions that can keep us from getting the right focus and gets us there quicker than pursuing it alone.

Having an established plan, a team of collaborating co-workers, and shared goals increases your chances of success.

When you have a partner, you typically meet more often to discuss business, you are frequently challenged, and you share goals and objectives for the project or work. Having someone to cheer for you and with you when you report progress and achievements is inspiring and will accelerate progress, build motivation, and bring results.

— CAROLINE GRØNVOLD, VP PRODUCT
& INNOVATION, HURTIGRUTEN

B *orn of a lust for adventure and a real desire to "make a difference," Hearts in the Ice and Hilde and Sunniva will go down in history as women who not only defied odds but contributed to the science of under-standing climate change in a most extraordinary way. This "contribution" is and will be invaluable. The importance of their contribution cannot be overlooked. Through their citizen-science projects and teaching opportuni-ties, they have exposed literally thousands of people to a stark reality that shapes the future of Svalbard and the world. They have also touched lives around the world, from people in cities on each continent to the smallest of communities (Comox Valley on Vancouver Island has a fan base that would rival any other). They are followed on social media; they are talked about at dinner tables; they are held up as models of success, perseverance, and commitment to sons, daughters, nieces, and nephews everywhere. Young and old see Hilde and Sunniva's achievements as inspiring and "extraor-dinary" at a time when what we do matters; they will be remembered by those whose future is shaped by our actions . . . or inaction.*

Sunniva and Hilde have shown us that dreams are not dead . . . that hope still exists, and that each of us . . . is the change that needs to happen.

— KATHLEEN URDAHL AND SHENA HINKS

I *think what makes what Hilde and Sunniva are doing extraordinary is why they are doing it. Too often people head off into the field with no purpose other than to say, "Been there, done that." It could easily have been enough for them to overwinter in the cabin and come back saying, "We were the first to women to overwinter solo," but that was never the primary mission. Their goal has always been to draw attention to our fragile polar regions, which are warming at twice the rate of the planet. They assembled an amazing team of experts, partnered with an incredible group of organiza-tions for citizen-science projects, and are sharing it with the general public and students around the world. At a time when a lot of people are talking about what is happening, Hilde and Sunniva have taken it ten steps further to document the problem in a way that no one else is doing.*

— JOE GRABOWSKI, FOUNDER/DIRECTOR,
EXPLORING BY THE SEAT OF YOUR PANTS

*C*reating global platforms to inform, inspire, share knowledge, and create a strong, united voice for (global) change is vital today.

Personally, the experience has been truly inspiring. It has shown that there are untraditional ways and platforms for sharing common passions, experiences, and knowledge. Hilde and Sunniva are hardworking and ensure that all partners and people involved are getting the most out of it, always finding genuine new opportunities. They are genuine in terms of making everyone feel special in their projects.

— BETINA RONDAN SOLLIE, FOUNDER,
COCO-MAT NORWAY

I think the future IS these types of collaborations. Hearts in the Ice is a shining example of bringing together a wide range of individuals, companies, organizations, and institutions to stand together for something that affects us all. The world needs more of these types of initiatives to keep bringing us together to work toward a common cause, especially one as important as the health of our planet.

— ERIC SACZUK, DRONE EXPERT, BRITISH COLUMBIA INSTITUTE
OF TECHNOLOGY

I have found it very inspiring during a particularly challenging time in my life. I have lived vicariously through them. Their experiences were so top-of-mind and touched me so much that I dedicated a month to painting the landscape around their cabin in the Norwegian Arctic as a gift to my friend Sunniva. Many people in my community have now seen this painting, and it has been the catalyst for many conversations about what Sunniva and Hilde are doing up north and why it is important. It has also stirred additional interest in their blog.

I think also that Covid-19 has to be mentioned here. Many people have had to undergo restrictions, isolation, a change in their lives, and have had to summon courage during the past six months, and Sunniva and Hilde have provided some lessons in their blog on how to cope with these things due to their own hardships, restrictions, and isolation.

— ANNABELLE JANE MURRAY, ARTIST

*I*t's important to encourage women to trust that they are worthy of their roles as leaders. To dare to challenge old systems and to think in new ways. To dare to stand up for what you believe—even if you meet resistance or face some "tough" situations. I belong to several networks with a majority of women—but I don't think too much about the fact that we are women when we're working together.

— HILDE BENDIXEN, SENIOR ADVISOR, NORGES BANK

*A*fter the Bamsebu project, I hope we can find ways of collaborating and building new bridges out to different parts of society too. Maybe inspire others to engage in citizen science and create a groundswell of desire to contribute.

It's important for the ideas to proliferate and spread far beyond the two fine ladies at Bamsebu. We must make a difference beyond ourselves. They show that anybody can make a difference if they just put their soul into it. Extraordinary determination, will, and desire to achieve something for the world.

—KIM HOLMÉN, INTERNATIONAL DIRECTOR,
NORWEGIAN POLAR INSTITUTE

A CALL TO ACTION FOR WOMEN

*W*e propose to learn from texts and numbers—data and its arrangement become the structure for teaching and learning. But what if we learned by example? By the fact of doing and achieving something that not only teaches but inspires. If this team had been all men, the entire program and its communication would have been different, more conventional and predictable. Yes, there is the proof of outer strength and ingenuity and discovery in the accomplishment, but there is also the revelation and *expression of inner strength, perhaps different values, certainly a revelatory discovery that speaks to the heart.*

— PETER NEILL, FOUNDER/DIRECTOR,
WORLD OCEAN OBSERVATORY

*F*ind your inner lioness; speak out. We make up half the world's population, yet we allow the male world to govern and destroy. We are running out of time.

— ESTHER GRANT

*H*earts in the Ice is proof that every girl, mother, and grandmother can carry with them the badge of courage and fearlessness. A badge that can't be seen but which we know we have and can reach to for confirmation and support when we might not be feeling so brave or powerful. I am grateful for the badge of courage that Hilde and Sunniva have gifted me and women across the world.

— BETTINA BRECKENFELD, SISTER EXTRAORDINAIRE

*D*o, rather than not doing . . . get involved, speak up, do your homework, read, and learn. Be part of our future and its outcomes for all.

— KAREN AUSTIN, CO-OWNER,
CREATIVE CONCEPTS DESIGN

*F*ind your passion! AND weave the four attributes within you so that as you become a fully expressed woman, you don't do so by pushing back against men or masculinity. We each have all four attributes in different "proportions"—women and men have equal value, but different job descriptions. Women need to step into their proper roles as leaders, as stewards of creation, and as guardians of our collectivity, but they need to do this without pushing men down. Women and men need to honor one another again.

— MARTI SPIEGELMAN, LEADERSHIP ADVISOR, MENTOR,
SPEAKER, FOUNDER, SELWYN HOUSE SCHOOL (INDIGENOUS INITIATION AND MENTORING PROGRAM)

*Y*ou can only stand to gain by giving things a shot.
— CAROLYN STROUD

*C*onnection and communication with ourselves and with others is the red thread. Live your own personal values. Clear, confident, credible.
Be an inspiration to others by doing what you say in everything you do. Do what you love and take care of body, mind, soul, children, friends, and passions.
In other words, be your own best leader; become sustainable!
— CARINA VINBERG, LEADERSHIP AND PERSONAL COACH

*T*rust who you are and your inner guts to be the woman you want to be. The future will be what we build today, so don't wait; make it happen.
— ANA ROSA MARISCAL, CORPORATE COMMUNICATIONS, BRP

*I*f you were men, I am sure you would have way more sponsors and press and way less impact because the story would be about triumph over nature. Your story is about coexisting and innovation and alignment of heart with purpose, and not everyone understands it in a sound bite.
— LIZ MACDONALD, SPACE WEATHER SCIENTIST, NASA

*T*he climate changes in the polar areas, and specifically in Svalbard, are by far the most important challenge we face at present. Knowledge, research, and debates are the only way to stop or minimize these processes and their severe effects. This is not a Svalbard issue but a big and complex global issue. I do, however, think that most people need to see the little picture in the big picture. The global picture is simply too big, but if you can manage to take it down to the narrower frame—two women, nature, changes—that is something most people can understand. This again will motivate your followers to understand the big and scarier picture.
— BØRGE DAMSGÅRD, PROFESSOR, MARINE BIOLOGY, THE UNIVERSITY CENTER IN SVALBARD

D are to be different, dare to say yes to opportunities and challenges—make sure you use your female strengths. Challenge imbalances in management at your work or in projects—bring the discussion to the table. Stand up for your rights, think big, and cultivate relationships. Find your mentors and make sure to capitalize on your network and connections.

— CAROLINE GRØNVOLD, VP PRODUCT
& INNOVATION, HURTIGRUTEN

Y ou are just as capable as any human on this planet. You are what you eat, so eat positivity. Don't let anyone convince you that all men want to see you fail. They don't. Victimhood is no good. You can do what the fuck you like; it's all up to you. Some will celebrate your triumphs; some won't. It's up to you to keep going or to rest; both of those things are okay. Don't let an outside opinion affect your opinion of yourself. You know what is right and wrong; stay strong. If you want to wear pink and roll around in glitter, do it! If you want to learn how to shoot a gun and spit tobacco balls, then do it. It really doesn't matter. Just live your life and don't put yourself in a box you never wanted to be in in the first place. You're a woman! Great, now go be a good human and pay no mind to the stereotypes that society gave you. A flower only survives if you water it; it's up to you what parts of your life and mind you want to water.

— JOSS STONE, SINGER, SONGWRITER

M other Nature needs her daughters.

— FABIAN DATTNER, LEADERSHIP EXPERT, FOUNDER,
HOMEWARD BOUND PROJECTS

I t is important for young girls and women to see themselves in any role they wish and to continue to break down any barriers in their way.

Engaging students one step at a time is the key. "Pole pole"—Swahili for "slowly"—just as Sunniva taught me on our six-day Kilimanjaro trek. One step at a time. Make a goal for each day of your climb versus looking at the peak and feeling overwhelmed and wondering how you will ever get there. It's an analogy for climate change too.

— SHARON COZENS, DIRECTOR OF ADVANCEMENT,
SELWYN HOUSE SCHOOL

*M*y experience on Svalbard at the launch of Hearts in the Ice—what I saw, the stories I heard, the people I met—all strengthened my resolve to take action, work for a better planet for my children, and find ways to help my community take up its leadership with regard to climate mitigation, adaption, and resilience in what is a time of great change.

— KAREN ELLIOTT, MAYOR, SQUAMISH, BRITISH COLUMBIA, CANADA

*I*t wouldn't be too much of a stretch to suggest that the "golden age of exploration and adventure" has come and gone. That is, until you reflect on what it is exactly that these two women have undertaken and achieved. When you conduct a search of those who have explored the polar regions of the world, you'll likely find that search lists only one, or possibly two women. What this tells you is that the harsh polar environments have been seen as the exclusive exploration grounds of men whose gender afforded them the luxury of support, encouragement, and, most importantly, funding. Funding for most things, including exploration, has always been tied to the calcu-lated risk of success or failure. For men, this has rarely been a barrier . . . for women, it's a different story. There is no question that advances in equality and access to pay equity have been made by women over the last four de-cades. But it is the truth that there continue to be barriers, limitations, and reduced expectations tied to the very stale and delusional belief that women are in some way inferior and cannot be tested the way men have been in difficult and dangerous circumstances. This has bred a desire in some women to take that outdated model of limitation and turn it on its head.

— KATHLEEN URDAHL AND SHENA HINKS

No one had ever done what we have now done—two women spending an entire winter on Svalbard without men. The history of trapping on Svalbard stretches back about 150 years and includes countless winter stays. And it's full of men. About men and written by men.

The Norwegian tradition of spending an entire winter in the Arctic started in earnest in the late nineteenth, early twentieth centuries when men from northern Norway who lived a simple life with few resources would often set off to make their way up north as trappers. They had few alternative ways to earn a living. The land in the far north of Svalbard was rich with resources like polar bears and foxes that could bring in a good return, and the men lived off the sea and land and dreamed of these riches. The transition from life on the mainland back then was not as extreme as it is now.

Today's lifestyle is very different—we live in abundance and quite removed from living directly off the land. In today's world, spending a winter on Svalbard involves giving up a whole lot more. You give up access to electricity and water, the internet and grocery stores, and easy access to communication, including with your loved ones. That's the price you pay for living simply and alongside nature. But undertaking a winter stay here on Svalbard is not the only way to live simply—there are many ways to go back in time.

We have lost a lot of the knowledge people had a hundred years ago, but fortunately, there are stories that have been shared through the generations, some of them even depicted in literature. There aren't enough women who have recorded their stories of time on Svalbard through the ages, but those who have recorded them have been incredibly inspirational. Here are some of their stories:

> The French writer **Léonie d'Aunet** was the first woman on Svalbard. As a nineteen-year-old, she accompanied her husband on the La Recherche Expedition in 1838.

> **Christiane Ritter** didn't like Svalbard when she arrived at Gråhuken one foggy day in 1934. She had left her four-year-old daughter, Karin, at home in Austria to spend the winter on Svalbard with her husband and another trapper named Karl. Luckily, the fog lifted, and her descriptions of the land, the colors, and the variety of light, seasons, and nature have been read by people over the whole world. She was mesmerized! The descriptions of the light and the fjords, mountains, and glaciers are vivid, beautiful, and detailed. While the men were out trapping during the Arctic night, she spent a lot of time alone, and she described how this affected her and how important work and activity were for her mental health. In her book, *A*

Woman in the Polar Night, she describes enduring an extended storm on her own, then writes, "What a godsend our fellow humans are."

Helfrid Nøis spent more time in the Arctic winter than any other woman and was responsible for leaving a feminine touch on an otherwise male-dominated world. Villa Fredheim, the trapper's cabin where her husband, Hilmar Nøis, had already spent many winters, bore the mark of the men who had lived there for many years: It was simple and practical, but not very cozy by a woman's standards. Helfrid turned the trapper's cabin into a home, painting the walls in the kitchen and living room in lively colors and creating upholstered sofas. She also ordered a new stove and lay nice rugs on all the floors, and soon, as Tor Jacobsen writes in *Ishavskinne: Historien om Helfrid Nøis* ("The Woman of the Arctic Ocean: The Story of Helfrid Nøis"), "the home smelled of bread and cakes. There was a tablecloth on the table at every meal and freshly pressed curtains on the windows."

Wanny Woldstad was Norway's first female taxi driver, as well as the first person in Norway to get a heater in her car. She lived in Tromsø, and in 1932, trapper and charmer Anders Sæterdal took a ride in her taxi. That same year, she accompanied him north on a trapping expedition. For five years she participated in trapping as the first female trapper—the first woman on men's "turf." Some felt threatened: The next winter, 1933–4, trapper Georg Bjønnes wrote a legal suggestion in his diary: "For winter trappers, the age limit should be set at twenty to sixty years old. Women and children should not, under any circumstances, be permitted to spend the winter in the trapping fields." It must have been hard for Wanny back then. A male author once remarked, "Women's inroads into trapping will weaken, and in the worst case, destroy the myth that spending the winter at a remote station far from people and with daily contact with wild animals and destructive nature is something only brave men can handle."

Wanny was a small woman, just 157 cm (5 feet 1 inch) tall, but she quickly learned the art of the hunt and often hunted alone. With time, she became just as effective a hunter as any man. There was a lot of heavy work, especially when there was a large polar bear to be skinned, cut up, and sent back to the station. Nonetheless, she describes her life as a trapper on Svalbard as "wonderful! In spite of the dangers, tension and struggles, it's an ideal way of life."

The book about Wanny, *The First Female Trapper on Svalbard*, has been an inspiration for Hilde. Wanny describes her experiences with nature and wildlife in a personal and simple manner. Her desire to care for wildlife, while at the same time reaping its benefits, is reflected through a genuine interest in and compassion and respect for all living creatures. And it was Wanny's writing that taught us to rotate our eggs regularly so they would keep for as long as possible. If the yolk oozes out through the egg white into the shell, the egg rots.

Hanna Resvoll-Holmsen was the first climate warrior and Norway's first accredited botanist. In 1907, she caught a ride with Prince Albert I of Monaco and spent a large portion of the summer alone on Svalbard, documenting the flowers and plant life that grew there. She would go on to spend several summers in the region, and her research and publications would become important to Norwegian sovereignty on Svalbard, with her contributions to the conservation of species and areas becoming part of the Svalbard Treaty that placed Svalbard under Norwegian sovereignty in 1920. She also became an important force in the struggle to preserve natural lands both on Svalbard and on mainland Norway. In 1973, thirty years after her death, three national parks, two nature reserves, and a series of bird sanctuaries were formed on Svalbard. On mainland Norway, Hanna fought against expanding the dams at Sjoa and Gjende. The Norwegian Parliament passed long-term preservation acts for Sjoa and Gjende in 1973, the same year protections were enacted on Svalbard. Hanna was also behind several large national parks in Norway, among them Dovre National Park.

THE DIFFERENCE BETWEEN WOMEN AND MEN

When Wanny and Helfrid came to Svalbard, the social differences between women and men were greater than they are today. Men's and women's roles were clearly defined: The men would trap and maintain their tools while the women made sure there was food on the table and maintained the home and clothing. As a thoroughly untraditional woman, Wanny was allowed to participate in trapping, but she also prepared meals and maintained the home—meaning that if a woman wanted to participate in the men's world, she had to do double the work. On mainland Norway, it was also common for women to undertake tasks of a physical nature that were ordinarily performed by men, like chopping wood and carrying water, while also dealing with everything else that was expected of them—namely, everything in the home. But before Wanny, a woman had never participated in trapping on Svalbard.

Today, women's and men's social roles are less clear-cut. Men contribute to traditionally female tasks such as taking care of the home, the children, and cooking, and thank goodness women go to work, participating in all areas that were formerly the domain of men alone.

And yet, the world still needs female leaders with traditional, feminine characteristics. Women have demonstrated throughout history that they can work double-time, shouldering both physical work and society's psychological and emotional needs. In most women's ways of operating in the world, showing vulnerability is not a weakness; it's a strength. Success has never been about bragging rights and accomplishments. What women might lack in physical strength, they make up for in their ability to solve problems creatively and collaborate. This has given women across the ages the ability to interact, show compassion, make decisions, and lead.

GIRL POWER

Still, women trying to rise into leadership roles face cultural and systemic hurdles such as unconscious bias, which makes it harder for them to advance. This doesn't apply only in business; it's true across most if not all industries and platforms. Traditionally, women have been taught to be competitive with each other (thank God for sports as an outlet!), perhaps because there truly have been fewer jobs for us at the top ranks, seeming to force us to fight over the ones that do exist. Supply and demand?

If the two of us had been men, we would have thumped on our chests a lot louder and harder and probably would have gotten more funding and sponsorship opportunities—but we wouldn't have cultivated and nurtured this incredibly diverse community of supporters, female and male. This network of badass leaders has meant more and holds more power and value than any amount of money.

Unconscious bias is everywhere, from the neighborhoods and close friends we choose to the people we date. Developments in neuroscience have now demonstrated that we form many biases throughout our lives—mainly through societal and parental conditioning—and hold them subconsciously.

We constantly gather millions of pieces of information, and our brains process that information in a certain way, unconsciously categorizing and formatting it into familiar patterns. Though most of us have difficulty accepting or acknowledging it, we all do it. Gender, ethnicity, disability, sexuality, body size, profession, and so on—all of these factors influence the assessments we make of people and form the basis of our relationships with others and the world at large.

There's power in relationships that extend beyond these generic first impressions. When you create connections based on shared interests and goals, you'll be more successful at your job, because let's face it, people want to work with people they know and like—and life's too short to work with people you *don't* really like. Simply putting yourself in environments that give you the opportunity to meet with peers, get to know each other, and share experiences can be a game changer. Chances are, if you make meaningful connections, they will last a lifetime. On this journey, we have looked at every science partner, sponsor, individual follower, media contact, and educational resource as a meaningful connection. We have sought to develop authentic exchanges with everyone we've encountered, and when we've been lucky enough to find mutuality, we have turned these encounters into lasting relationships. A relationship touches your heart and creates an everlasting partnership—but if you want to keep connections alive, they must be nurtured.

Together, we are stronger.

So, from the bottom of our hearts, we thank our Girl Power team:

Sandy O'Keefe for our website; Fabian Dattner at Homeward Bound; Ellen Kvam at Ellen Kvam Norwegian Design; Linda McCormick at Borton Overseas; Ana Rosa Mariscal and Leslie Quinton at Bombardier Recreational Products; Carina Vinberg at Framgångare; Kit Jackson at Strategy Together; Kalina Leling at Iridium; Wenche Skjellnan at Det Lille Under; Caroline Grønvold at Hurtigruten; Monica Paulsen at Negotia; Flin MacDonald at Centric; Camilla Hagen Sørli at Canica; Kate, Jo, and Jessika at Marlink; Allison Lee at Scripps; Liz MacDonald at NASA; Janne and Vanessa at UNIS; Marilé at NASA; Gro at Devold; Kathrine at Grønt Maskin; Randi at Felleskjøpet; Caroleigh at Klean Kanteen; Martine at Chooose; Hilde at Hansen Protection; Betina at COCO-MAT; Signe from Skinnboden in Longyearbyen; Camilla at The North Face; Marion at Arc'teryx; Maria Philippa; Pascale Lortie; Lea; Vera; Anne-Margrethe; Bente; Susanne; Brit; Liv Hege; Anne-Lise; Elin B.; Elin W.; Anne Mette; Hege; Bettina B.; Maren B.; Karen E.; Ellice; Keitha S.; Esther, Karen; Shena; Jody F.; Rosie B.; Sharon C.; Kathy N.; Kathryn S.; Kathleen U.; Maureen M.; Caroline S.; Marti S.; Annette B.; Hilde B.; Anne M.; Joss Stone.

Colliding lights.

Drift ice and glacier ice.

Bamsebu and Ettra, Pettra.

Reindeer at sunset, facing north west toward Malbukta.

Sunniva and Ettra hiking from Kapp Fleur de Lys.

The magic pastel light of Svalbard in February.

Indrorobotics drone test.

Reindeer looking right at us (springtime, after the snow has melted).

Polar bear mum (N26131) with her four-month cub.

Arctic fox, just outside Bamsebu.
Fun fact:They have the warmest fur known to man/woman!

The moon shining bright outside.

In front of Nathorst glacier—after polar bear sightings.

Practicing our yoga poses.

Outdoor BBQ on the Tundra on the 17th Mai!

Ettra with the Northern Lights and beautiful moon in the background.

Bamsebu, 140 km from Longyearbyen.

The team and two riverboats with slush ice forming in the fjord.

Magical February light at Kapp Fleur de Lys.

First snowmobile trip with our Lynx in October 2019.

Drone footage from a skitrip to Richardodden. Summer 2019 setup.

Basecamp Bamsebu with solar panels, food barrels, sauna, our Lynx, and Ettra.

Hilde and Ettra after a trip to Kapp Fleur de Lys.

CHAPTER 11

DRIVING ACTION AND

PROMOTING ENGAGEMENT

Tell me, what is it you plan to do with your one wild and precious life?
— Mary Oliver

As a mission-driven project, *Hearts in the Ice* is not out to save the world, but we are here as two strong leaders to say that the world needs saving.

Today's corporate climate movement centers on how companies can do less harm. This is a start, but it is clearly not enough.

As the gatekeepers of progress on the climate crisis, large corporations must use their power and broaden their view on what the climate crisis is really about. If they only view the crisis through their own lenses and the damage they can minimize, they will only see a small slice of the available solutions.

Collaboration is essential—both internally and externally. At the end of the day, it boils down to you and me and our values. Who are we, what are we doing, what are our choices and which solutions do we decide to pursue? What will it take for all of us to be changemakers?

Every business must now ask not only, "How can we reduce our emissions as quickly as possible?" but also, "How can we use our full resources, scale, influence, and the passion of our employees and the broader community to help build a world where all living things can thrive?"

Goals are crucial because they govern direction and define what we are reaching for and the resources needed to get there. They're also the primary way most businesses articulate their climate ambitions.

We went through our own process of goal setting for this project. When we started *Hearts in the Ice*, we had a passionate interest in education, awareness, and engagement. We asked ourselves, "How can we, as two individuals, create a movement that will drive impactful change around this climate crisis, one person at a time?" To answer that question, we first drew on our backgrounds and experience, our networks, and the stories we could tell about changes we had both seen in the polar regions over a span of more than two decades. We then laid out three tiers of goals within our overarching plan. Both of us are good at generating ideas, but we didn't work alone: We sought out expert help in crafting a strategy that would assist us in realizing our goals. For this, we have a few people to thank, including Kit from Strategy Together, Carina from Framgångare, and Fabian from Homeward Bound. Teamwork creates dreamwork. Collaboration was essential!

The current gold standard of corporate climate goals—net zero by several decades from now—is insufficient to the scale of the problem. This kind of long-term target would only be adequate if every company on Earth not only made the same commitment but achieved it before the deadline—a highly unlikely prospect.

More expansive and ambitious goal setting can articulate things like how businesses plan to show up for their communities, get involved in zoning and city planning, and create resilience and engagement in their employees and communities. We need civic engagement in which each person feels valued and each person understands that they have an active role to play as corporate citizens and stewards of Earth.

We all know the basics: When we burn fossil fuels (coal, oil, and natural gas), manufacture cement, plough rich soils, and destroy forests, we release heat-trapping carbon dioxide into the air. "Drawdown," meanwhile, refers to the potential for removing carbon dioxide from the atmosphere through innovative land-use practices, regenerative agriculture, and agroforestry—an agricultural system that mimics the forests. Paul

Hawken wrote a comprehensive book on this very concept: *Drawdown: The Most Comprehensive Plan Ever Proposed to Reverse Global Warming.* It's a testament to the growing stream of humanity that understands the enormity of the challenges we face and is willing to devote their lives to a future of kindness, security, and regeneration.

We can also apply the ideas and concepts of drawdown to illuminate ways to overcome the fear, confusion, and apathy surrounding climate change. Because we don't just need to achieve drawdown—the moment when atmospheric levels of greenhouse gasses peak and begin to decline. We also need to build a world where we can sustain it.

This requires not only technological solutions, but also social and cultural changes and relational, community-building work to carry us forward. And there are so many people who want to contribute. Given how all-encompassing the issue is—how big and complex and interrelated—how is it that only a handful of people with "sustainability" in their titles get to work on these issues in their day jobs? In this, the greatest, most all-encompassing challenge any generation has ever faced, every job can and should be a climate care job. Every person on the planet can become a citizen scientist, an activist, or an engaged steward by finding a thing or issue they are passionate about and getting involved in it.

We need deep engagement inside company walls and activism on the streets so that employees can be activists and activists can be employees. To use the tagline from the Canadian manufacturer BRP: "Together We Ride." Our employers shouldn't dampen the strength of our pushing and the ferocity of our fighting, but instead welcome and encourage it. Beyond our places of employment, we all have our eyes on the same goal and are marching or riding toward it together.

There is no one-size-fits-all solution to the climate crisis, as much as we wish there was. It spills over into every aspect of life, so responding to it with a narrow lens won't work. We all need to broaden our scopes and understand that self-leadership, expansiveness of thought, and problem-solving are the only ways forward.

Let's take a more detailed look at the problem and why we each need to collaborate to lead the charge right now.

There have been some efforts at the national level to address the most immediate pollution problems, but the regulation of CO2 emissions has been anemic at best. Global warming is an existential threat to all of humanity, and it's not being met with the necessary leadership or urgency.

The Paris Agreement was a positive development and, at the time, a big step toward addressing this most vexing of issues. It appeared as if the world was coming together to achieve the required changes. The countries involved were rising to the challenge in a spirit of cooperation and innovation, and things were at last headed in the right direction. But things essentially fell apart after the United States pulled out of the Paris Agreement and the UN Climate Change Conference COP 25 in 2019, and by then it was clear that international cooperation had reached its limits.

Nevertheless, there were some positive signs. In 2019, global CO_2 emissions from energy production plateaued at around 33 gigatonnes (Gt), after two years of increases. The main contributing factor was a sharp drop in CO_2 emissions that resulted from the way power was being produced in advanced economies, which were increasingly using renewable sources (mainly wind and solar) as well as switching their fuel source from coal to natural gas and using more nuclear power.

Then came even more cause for hope in the form of a new president and vice president for the United States. In his inaugural address, President Joe Biden said, "A cry for survival comes from the planet itself. A cry that can't be any more desperate or any more clear now." He then signed an executive order on his first day in office, reversing the withdrawal from the Paris Agreement ordered by his predecessor, Donald Trump. The US rejoined the agreement 107 days after pulling out.

Meanwhile, not a day goes by without further proof that human activity is drastically altering ecozystems and that the changes are having dire impacts across the globe. In the words of Christiana Figueres, Former Executive Director of the UN Framework Convention on Climate Change, when the Paris Agreement was reached, "We must all become stubborn optimists." We are facing an existential threat, and we are not responding adequately to the challenges. No single industrial nation is on track to meet its Paris commitments, and two degrees of warming now looks like a best-case outcome, with an entire bell curve of more horrific possibilities.

Two degrees of warming has been considered the threshold of catastrophe: flooded cities, crippling droughts and heatwaves, a planet hammered daily by monsoons and hurricanes. But there is now no possibility that change will be limited to that best-case outcome. Since the Kyoto

Protocol was signed some twenty years ago, CO2 emissions have risen sharply.

Take Australia, for example, which in the last few years has experienced its most devastating wildfires ever—while being governed by a prime minister who is a noted climate sceptic elected with the support of the coal industry, which is the country's leading source of export revenues. The situation is almost surreal: The country has been devastated, and the political leadership hasn't even acknowledged the root of the problem.

It's not as though solutions aren't available. They are—and there are increasing signs that they're cost-efficient too. However, the current set of nationally determined contributions as laid out in the Paris Agreement is wholly insufficient. Even if they were fully implemented, we would be on track to reach a temperature rise of at least three degrees Celsius.

Young people are demanding that governments take climate change far more seriously and force more progress. But we need action from, and for, everyone in multiple areas of society—including compulsory education on these topics both nationally and internationally. In the words of Kathleen Rogers, President of Earth Day Network: "Young people, through movements such as Fridays for Future, have been asking governments to tell the truth about the climate and environmental emergencies that we are now facing—'telling the truth' needs to happen in the schools and universities, and needs to happen now."

"Throughout history, many great morally based movements have gained traction at the very moment when young people decided to make that movement their cause," Al Gore said when interviewed for a *TIME* magazine article profiling Greta Thunberg. In many ways, Greta personifies the angst of a generation that is growing up in an uncertain world. When she first learned of the effects of climate change at school in a video depicting starving polar bears, extreme weather, and flooding, she sank into a deep depression and didn't really snap out of it until she sat down in front of the Swedish Parliament with her SKOLSTREJK FÖR KLIMATET sign on August 20, 2018. Doing something—taking a stand—felt better than doing nothing. Here are a few of our favorite quotes from the journey that followed for Greta:

> "Learning about climate change triggered my depression
> in the first place. But it was also what got me out of my

depression because there were things I could do to improve the situation."

"We can't just continue living as if there was no tomorrow because there is a tomorrow."

"I want you to panic. I want you to feel the fear I feel every day. And then I want you to act."

Greta's lonely strike outside the Swedish Parliament went exponential and coincided with (or precipitated) a surge of mass youth protests that have erupted around the world, in different areas, with different impacts, but all fueled by social and environmental instability and economic pressures. The children of this world are inheriting a raw deal and are recognizing that older generations are irresponsible stewards of the world that they will leave to future generations. Children should not have to be responsible for the problems for which our generation should have been held to account. Short-term political expediency, rampant corruption, and ignorance are not the way to manage global affairs. Global leadership has shown a blatant disregard for the well-being of the planet and future generations, and Greta has called them out on it.

As Executive Secretary of the UN Framework Convention on Climate Change (UNFCC), Patricia Espinosa has welcomed initiatives from Mexico and Italy to ramp up their climate and environmental education as part of their climate-change response, describing this commitment as a key contribution to the countries' climate commitments. "Climate change should be included in school curricula and should play a central role in updated Nationally Determined Contributions," she noted. "I look forward to more countries factoring in climate education into their national climate action plans." Martha Delgado Peralta, Vice Minister of Multilateral Affairs and Human Rights, Mexican Ministry of Foreign Affairs, has added: "Great transformations can only be achieved through knowledge, awareness, and the sense of collaboration. We are convinced that environmental education is the route to meeting Sustainable Development Goals, an essential tool to fight the climate crisis and can prompt a profound cultural change to contribute to our planet's sustainability."

So how did we get here? In the 1970s, capitalizm went off the rails with the rise of shareholder primacy and businesses not paying attention to their other stakeholders, including their employees and communities. In the past few years, the flaws in this model have been readily apparent, and the escalation of environmental concerns has made it clear that businesses must be held accountable for their conduct. What is the company's value chain? How does it make its products? Are they sustainably produced? What are the ethics behind the company's management? In 2019, there was a lot of talk about responsible corporate capitalism, but now, we need action. Businesses that fail to change and try to pursue business as usual will be left behind.

Achieving carbon neutrality will require a complete transformation of the economy. It means rethinking policies on clean energy, industry, patterns of production and consumption, transport, food and farming, and construction. All human economic development has been built on the exploitation of fossil fuels, so eliminating them from our daily lives is an almighty undertaking. Take oil, for instance. The world consumes 100 million barrels of oil per day. The world runs on this substance: It provides more of our energy than any other source—34 percent, followed by coal at 27 percent and natural gas at 24 percent. Oil is also used in many of the products that we use daily, including paint, washing detergents, nail polish, plastics, medical equipment, mattress foams, clothing, coatings for TV screens, and more. But not all oil is equally destructive, and as we transition away from this fossil fuel, we need to ensure that the oil we do use is as low in carbon as possible. The Johan Sverdrup oil field in Norway has one of the lowest carbon rates in the world.

What is required is better energy. Renewables, yes! But they are still a relatively small component of the total energy mix and not yet a complete solution. Punishing energy companies for being in business is not the way forward, as they will be key drivers of innovation and the transition to a more sustainable future. Meanwhile, all industries and businesses need to improve efficiency, innovate, and rethink the way they conduct their business. Governments, the UN, international organizations, civil society, businesses, investors, and individuals must all do everything in their power to act and address this existential threat and to provide and use better, cleaner energy. We're all in this together, and we all need to be part of the solution. We all need to start adopting expedition behavior.

History reveals that, through human ingenuity, we have been able to achieve remarkable things. We would like to be stubborn optimists and insist that humanity will solve our carbon problem before life on this planet is wiped out, but we are on a very dangerous path. We do not know how Earth's ecozystems will respond to the pressures we are placing on them. The changes in the natural world are happening faster and more dramatically than expected, and things might get much worse than anticipated. This challenge will only be met through innovation, engagement, and collaboration. We call upon teachers and leaders to help individuals and organizations meet their goals by helping them to learn, innovate, and change.

Though we never thought of ourselves as activists, we now see that we are in our role as citizen scientists. Our role as bridge builders between researchers and citizens is one drop in the bucket—but a necessary one. After all, if nobody understands the data and research, how in the world can we make informed decisions? That's why we encourage everyone reading this to learn to understand policy and advocate for citizen science to be recognized and subsidized as a way to collect data and engage communities. It is so easy to feel paralyzed by the facts presented, so we at *Hearts in the Ice* will stay positive and work even harder to inspire people to take action.

No place in the world will escape the impact of climate change—but we still don't really know what we know or have a good system for gathering salient data.

We have the tools, and we have the ability to leverage resources to gather more salient data globally so that all peoples are represented, but this will require collaboration between companies and governments across borders and cultures.

Our *Hearts in the Ice* community is your community. There can only be power in numbers—in all of us working together, toward stopping the escalation of climate change.

CHAPTER 12

LESS IS MORE

Experiment with Living Simply!

*The salvation of this human world lies nowhere else than in the
human heart, in the human power to reflect, in human modesty, and
in human responsibility. Without a global revolution in the sphere
of human consciousness, nothing will change for the better.*
— Václav Havel

Research into the brain and quantum physics point to how much power
we really have over our thoughts and habits—if only we focus our attention in the right places. But what does all that to do with climate change
and our choices? Just about everything.

Changing behavior is hard, even on the individual scale. One study
found that only one in nine people who underwent heart surgery was able
to change their lifestyle, despite having the ultimate motivation: possible
death. Facilitating change on the scale of a whole culture is even harder.

But as the new science of the brain has revealed, energy flows where
attention goes. At the heart of this framework is the idea that it is attention itself that changes the brain. At rest, our brains are noisy and full of

thoughts, like an orchestra warming up; all sorts of noises take over. But when we pay close attention to something, it's like taking all the chaotic orchestra sounds and bringing them together to play a lovely piece of music. Each individual player is in synch with the others—or, on the level of the brain, all thoughts are in synch.

So, when you pay close attention to something, multiple regions of your brain connect into a larger circuit to complete a specific task. When different circuits fire simultaneously, you invoke what is known as Hebb's rule, which Dr David Rock discusses in his book *Your Brain at Work: Strategies for Overcoming Distraction, Regaining Focus, and Working Smarter All Day Long*. The theory is that "cells that fire together, wire together"—which explains how paying close attention to an idea, an activity, a habit, or an experience helps create networks in the brain that can stay with you, wired together, sometimes forever.

All of which means that the brain is mutable, and it's changing all the time. It changes based on the lighting around you, the weather, what you eat, how you sit, and whom you talk to. The brain is happy to change—it's the attention span that is often not so happy to switch gears. As Sir Winston Churchill said, "I am always ready to learn, although I do not always like being taught." But when you manage to change what you pay attention to, you are rewiring your own brain. Right now, all humans need to rewire our habits and behaviors to be less consumer-driven—and these changes need to come from each of us. Nobody is ever motivated to change because someone else says they should or because someone tries to convince them it would be good for them.

This could be a good time to experiment with living differently since many routines and habits have been upended through the pandemic. And as you rewire your own routines and patterns, there's an opportunity to dig into your own true values. Look at the choices you make or don't make. Look at the food you eat—where does it come from, what's in the package, how much of it is processed? How much packaging is there? Think about your interests: What are your passions? What are you curious about? Are you living in alignment with your values? Are you giving to this planet or taking? Look at how you're showing up for your family, your friends, your co-workers. Look at how much water you're using. Look at how involved you are or are not in your community.

We've been asked many times in interviews over the past year how in the world we survived and thrived at Bamsebu with apparently so very little. How did we adapt and cope under extreme working and living conditions? What constitutes psychological resilience? How can a person live with intention, a small footprint, and less waste? What have we learned that might benefit others? ·

Here are just a few of the ideas WE came up with that YOU (dear reader) can effectively put into place.

Food storage/waste

At Bamsebu, we ate everything we made—there was almost no waste. We had a limited supply of fresh fruits and vegetables, and after that, we ate canned and frozen foods (we had a small freezer) and items purchased in bulk. We made sure to ask all suppliers to limit packaging so that we had minimal plastic and paper waste; some did, some didn't.

We had to carefully rotate fresh food so that it didn't spoil or freeze (a constant, vigilant process) because we had no refrigerator. Did you know that the CFCs and HCFCs (chlorofluorocarbons and hydrochlorofluorocarbons) used in refrigerators and air conditioners were largely responsible for depleting the ozone layer? Thanks to the 1987 Montreal Protocol, CFCs and HCFCs have largely been phased out, but many refrigerators that are still in circulation have these chemicals in the coolant—and they have the capacity to warm the atmosphere *1,000 to 9,000 times* more than carbon dioxide. Yikes! That makes them some of the most potent greenhouse gasses known to humankind. The problem is disposal, when most of the gasses are released—and it's a problem that needs to be addressed both locally and globally.

As for waste: Did you know that a third of all food raised or prepared does not make it from farm to factory to fork? Consumers throw out up to 35 percent of food in high-income economies, while low-income families waste very little. Now consider that about 800 million people worldwide are living with hunger and that the food we waste around the world contributes about 8 percent of greenhouse gas emissions.

How do we tackle this problem? In higher-income regions, major interventions are needed at the retail and consumer levels. The most important step is to preempt food waste before it happens for the greatest reduction of upstream emissions, then to reallocate unwanted food for human consumption elsewhere or another reuse, such as composting. Composting is one of the best ways to use food waste.

There was no option to compost at Bamsebu, so we tossed our very minimal food waste from cooking into the open sea (when we had an open sea). Otherwise, we stored it in a bear-proof barrel until we could safely dispose of it.

Food sourcing

When we did run out of fresh fruits or vegetables, making a special meal required time and creativity, but we did it! We would always light a candle and eat our meals together.

We had onions, cabbage, garlic, and apples that we peeled and froze when they were about to spoil.

We tried to eat green and as sustainably as possible, though the lack of fresh greens made this a challenge. We did treat ourselves to healthy smoothies made of kale, beets, almonds, berry powder, dates, frozen fruits, chia, flax, and coconut milk—most of it in powder form.

The food we sourced was sustainably caught or grown and organic. The fish we ate was caught in Svalbard, as was the Svalbard reindeer meat we ate.

We had no access to a store to replenish our supplies, but we learned that food lasts a lot longer than its date stamp. For example, our eggs lasted six months beyond the "best by" date, partly because we kept them cold and turned them every week, just like the trapper Wanny Woldstad did back in the 1930s.

Did you know that there are no standards for the date labeling on food packaging? The stamps indicating the "best before" and "sell by" dates are unregulated and confusing, and we urgently need consumer education to avoid excess waste. Some of that education so far has taken the form of campaigns celebrating ugly produce and efforts like Feeding the 5000—large public feasts made entirely from food that was nearly wasted. These events have been held in London, Paris, Dublin, Sydney, Amsterdam, Washington, DC, and Brussels. Before you go grocery shopping again, see what you can use in your fridge that might be spoiling soon.

Get creative and think *less waste.*

Alternative energy

We teamed up with the Norwegian climate company CHOOOSE to not just offset our carbon emissions, but offset *more* emissions than our expedition left behind, making it not only climate neutral but "climate positive." CHOOOSE buys carbon credits with Gold Standard verification directly from hand-picked projects in developing countries, helping to replace coal and oil with renewable energy in UN-verified countries. Additionally, all projects CHOOOSE supports correspond to three of the UN's seventeen sustainable development goals, meaning they provide additional benefits for the local population, such as clean water, better sanitary conditions, schooling, and more.

We were entirely off-grid at Bamsebu. There were no power lines, and the old trapper's cabin had never before had any power, so the challenge was on. We didn't need that much energy, but access to some was vital to the work we were doing.

Our primary energy sources were solar and wind power that charged four large batteries in a Power Controls power bank, via a Rutland wind turbine and two large solar panels. We used this power for small LED lights inside the cabin, which felt like an absolute luxury to read and write by. In the many months of total darkness during the polar night, having artificial light was a savior, both mentally and physically. We also had five exterior LED sensor lights for safety, and we used power to charge our Thales MissionLINK satellite, Iridium satellite phone, laptops, weather station, headlamps, camera and video batteries, night vision scope, speakers for music, and GPS.

How does all this apply to life away from Bamsebu? Off-grid rooftop solar panels can bring green electricity to remote regions and low-income areas and could eventually eliminate the need for large-scale centralized power grids. Imagine all the rural regions that could benefit from a lot of new jobs in renewable energy, re-energizing the local economy while helping regions adopt clean energy, such as solar.

As for lighting: Artificial light plays a huge role in everyone's day-to-day life, even outside of the polar night. It extends activity into the dark hours (or months) and also expands the spaces we can venture into. In fact, lighting is now so hardwired into human life that it accounts for 15 percent of all global electricity use!

LEDs are a great way to bring that electricity use down. Though still expensive compared to other lighting—presenting a barrier for low-income families—they're slowly coming down in price, and the longevity and energy efficiency offset the higher initial cost. If an LED bulb is turned on for five hours a day, it will last for twenty-seven years, and when an LED light is turned on, it uses 90 percent less energy than an incandescent light bulb! For people not connected to an electrical grid, solar LED lights can have a huge beneficial impact on economic livelihoods. And LEDs can be "tuned" to provide benefits to humans, such as greater alertness on highways or sleep inducement in residential neighborhoods. They can also benefit wildlife by preventing birds and turtles, for example, from being disoriented by artificial light.

Wind energy is at the forefront of initiatives to address global warming in the coming three decades. Second only to eliminating coolants from refrigerators and how we dispose of them in total impact. Windmills and where to put them is an extremely divisive topic since many people don't want wind farms in or near their neighborhoods. At Bamsebu, the wind blew almost all the time, meaning that our wind turbine was constantly active, producing energy for our power needs.

Human beings have harnessed the power of wind for millennia, capturing breezes, gusts, and gales to send mariners and their cargo down rivers and across seas. Wind farms have small footprints, typically using no more than 1 percent of the land they sit on, so farming, recreation, and other land uses can happen even while power is being generated.

But wind energy, like all energy sources, is part of a system, and if we want to grow that system, it's essential to invest in energy storage, infrastructure, distribution, and how to manage the waste when they are no longer operable.

Water

Ever wonder what it's like not to shower for close to nine months?

We'll spare you the gruesome details—let's just say that the first shower after we got back to Longyearbyen was divine! Without daily showers, our skin and hair had a chance to renew themselves, since frequent showering actually dries you out and robs your body of the oils its needs. Still, we couldn't have been more grateful for running water and that first hot shower. At Bamsebu, we had no running water or plumbing—no kitchen sink, no knobs to turn, no real toilet, no shower, no bathtub, no dishwasher, no washing machine. Nada.

We managed with about ten large thirty-gallon containers of fresh water that sat outside, frozen; one large intermediate bulk container (IBC) with 800 litres of fresh water that was also frozen; and, of course, chunks of ice that drifted in from the glacier with the currents and snow that we could collect and melt. Water was a precious resource, and we used it sparingly.

Using water at home consumes so much energy, and we waste so much of it. It takes energy to clean and transport it, to heat it, and to transport the wastewater afterwards. Did you know that the average American household uses roughly 303 litres (80 gallons) of water per day? Roughly 60 percent of that is for indoor use like toilets, showers, and washing machines, and roughly 30 percent is for outdoors and watering lawns. About 10 percent is lost to leaks.

For comparison, at Bamsebu, we used roughly 15–18 litres (4–5 gallons) per day between us. Granted, we were living in an extreme situation, entirely off the grid, but the difference still gives pause around how much water anyone really needs to use.

We washed our hair in a small rectangular bucket and then reused that water to wash our clothes. We tried to use snow whenever possible for washing dishes and keep the fresh water to cook with and drink. We had an outhouse, so there was no plumbing for the toilet. We burned the toilet paper and disposed of our human waste.

How does this apply back in the civilized world? There are a few ways to cut back on water usage indoors. We can install low-flush toilets, water-efficient washing machines, and low-flow faucets and shower heads. According to what we read in the book Drawdown, in the US, the Environmental Protection Agency (EPA) estimates that if one household out of every hundred swapped out their older toilet for a low-flow one, the country would save more than 38 million kWh (kilowatt hours) of electricity—enough to power 43,000 households for a month. If it's possible where you live, you could even consider a Cinderella incineration toilet, which uses a combustion process instead of water to get rid of waste.

Mental and physical health

We can't take care of each other or our planet if we don't take care of ourselves. In our case, living in isolation and darkness had its challenges, and the period of total darkness from November through February had a significant effect on our sleep and overall well-being. A lack of light intensity has been associated with decreased melatonin, which affects physiological rhythms related to energy, cognitive performance, and mood. We couldn't have survived nine months at Bamsebu—or twelve, as it ended up being—without some routine and tools to draw from that helped us cope and stay healthy.

We both like massages, face masks, pedicures, salt scrubs, training, and washing our hair. So, when we needed it, we would help each other and ourselves out by having a "spa" day—a day all about self-care, which would boost our morale, breed self-respect, and allow us to have some fun.

We trained six days a week in a very small space. It would be easy to replicate this at home: Just get a workout buddy (even a virtual one), make a goal, lose weight, and get stronger. We didn't get sick at all during our stay!

We got out for walks with Ettra every single day, regardless of the weather.

We kept a routine around our drone flying, cloud and aurora observation, and ice-core sampling. Our citizen-science projects gave us meaning and purpose. We slept on COCO-MAT organic mattresses, pillows, and duvets—innovative sleep products inspired by nature. Without a good night's sleep, we couldn't function effectively, and this would have impacted our decision-making, safety, and creativity.

Yoga was also key for us. Thirty minutes a day we would show up on the mat! And breathe. When we could, we would also run out on the frozen tundra or the ice with gaiters, headlamps, flare gun, and all. Other times of the year, we'd run on the bare tundra or the beaches.

Being so very isolated meant there was no external stimulation, so we had to be resourceful and rely on each other. Our ability to do this had huge implications for our well-being and our capacity to problem-solve positively and creatively. Being so far away from family and friends, staying connected was key. We had our satellite equipment that, though super expensive, enabled us to email and make phone calls. Video was never an option with the minimal download and upload speeds.

Our self-imposed isolation also gave us great respect for every single resource, thought, and action we took. Finding time to sit and be still breeds connection to that great thing we call creativity. As important as it is to be connected and wired to information, it's just as important to take the time to disconnect from social media. To connect with your own ideas and original thought.

CHAPTER 13

THERE IS HOPE

A PATH FORWARD

The ancestor of every action is a thought.
— Ralph Waldo Emerson

*R*estless: The way you feel when an idea overtakes you and fills your thoughts—morning, noon, and night. It's a bit like falling in love: all-consuming at first. And it's exactly how we felt from the moment we started discussing overwintering at Bamsebu.

We knew our dream was finally becoming a reality when we decided to charter the MS *Nordstjernen* and invite a hundred friends, family, science partners, and sponsors on a four-day send-off trip that would leave Longyearbyen on September 13, 2019, and drop us off at Bamsebu the next day, along with Ettra and a ship's worth of supplies and equipment.

But what was the journey to that point like? Before we even had a departure date, we had a rough idea of which month we would leave, as everything was driven by weather and when we could get transport. We also needed at least six weeks together to sort through supplies, lists, clothing, and logistics—list after list after list.

For many people, the thought of leaving a secure income, secure job, and secure home would be an absolute no-go. Too risky. Too vulnerable. It filled us with fear at times too—especially since we were both completely committed to our jobs in the expedition cruise industry—but the business of packing up our lives kept the insecurity at bay. We felt so confident about what we were doing. The confidence came from deeply rooted intuition and from knowing that we were about to embark on something most people only dream about. This was us, living with purpose. If not now, when?

With our sleeves rolled up, we embarked on the adventure of a lifetime—to successfully overwinter in Svalbard. If we hadn't had such faith in what we were doing, we might never have made it to Bamsebu. We had to raise close to 1.5 million kroner (roughly $166,000) to complete the entire project. We wrote emails early in the morning, late at night, and all weekend—just ask our friends and family, who barely saw us for the year before we left. We received our fair share of *no's* and form responses thanking us for our proposal—but, "no, thank you." But we never, never gave up. Just like the makers of the Netflix show *The Queen's Gambit*, who went through twenty years of rejections. "No one would be interested in chess," said producer after producer to the writer of the script. Then one day, it was picked up by a major network. The lesson? Never, never, never give up. Have faith in what you're doing, even if other people can't see the value in it yet. In our case, after a while, all of our "sponsor asks" became a bit of a game. When we got a no, thank you, we would simply get creative and fine-tune our pitch even more.

We came up with the name *Hearts in the Ice* as it spoke so clearly to us and our love for the polar regions. Then it was the logo—what should it be? A globe? A heart? A polar bear? We asked several people to come up with samples and sketches before eventually landing on Espen Andre Øverdahl's proposal of an "H" representing two bodies with outstretched hands, from pole to pole.

Next, we needed a website, which would be the face we presented to the world and detail the who, why, what, when, and how of our project. We reached out to people whom we knew could help us define the what and why. Every idea, every piece of input helped. We were like sponges for any word, idea, Post-it note, and suggestion that could help us move the project forward—which means there are far too many people to thank for their input. Then Sandy came into the picture, and a website was born.

Now we had a rough plan—but still, neither of us could comprehend how quickly things would grow. Momentum was building, and in a short time, our work grew from a small project into a movement that included people from all over the world.

So, what were our objectives? One of our main goals at Bamsebu was to really "live the experience" and be fully immersed in our nine months alone together, living a life that was remote, simple, isolated, and self-sufficient. Of course, another main goal was to live to tell about it.

We also wanted to create meaningful stories around the citizen-science projects we were doing and engage kids and adults around the world. But how? A regular satellite unit wouldn't work: We were too far north, and there was a huge mountain range in the way of transmission. We called everyone we knew and researched until we found a provider willing to help us. We were told that the Iridium Certus system would work and that there was a new, hot-off-the-press device called a Thales MCD-MissionLINK that we could use, if we could get one in time. Time was running out. In the end, we became the first civilians to test and use this unit that was built into a watertight Pelican case, weighing 20 kg (44 lbs) in total. The MCD arrived in Longyearbyen just days before our departure.

We had a robust advisory board, but the entire base of the project was driven by us—a team of two! Our strengths lay in our passionate desire to make a difference, our openness to ideas from the advisory board and other stakeholders, and our ability to weave together ideas and people across industries and platforms. This doesn't happen overnight—it's the culmination of decades of experience and the understanding that everything you've done in your life—the good and the bad—matters.

We used leadership tools to support our journey and make the most of our experience and impact. This project gave us both an opportunity to reflect and build awareness about ourselves—for instance, how we are perceived by others vs. how we see ourselves. This helped us to understand each other better, to support and encourage each other, and to grow. We took a hard look at how we got to where we are—what had worked and what had not. We took inventory of our skills, wishes, and goals, and created a strategic, focused path for moving forward. As we decided how to move forward and co-create the future, it was essential to know who we were and what we valued.

All in all, you can see that our journey to Bamsebu was a twisty, winding road! Creating *Hearts in the Ice* involved sending out many proposals, sitting in countless meetings, and asking for a lot of help—to the point that asking for help and support became one of the skills we're proudest of. It was clear to us from the beginning that our project was far greater than just the two of us. That made it easier to ask for help. But we also had to know ourselves, what we value, and what we stand for, and ask ourselves why this matters and why anyone else should care too. We had to draw a strategy map outlining where we wanted to go as well as how and why. And we had to step into being stronger and better leaders.

If you too are considering a bold plan, know that anything is possible. Just start, as we did, by drafting a plan on a piece of paper. Just start.

Explanation of the *Hearts in the Ice* Strategy Map

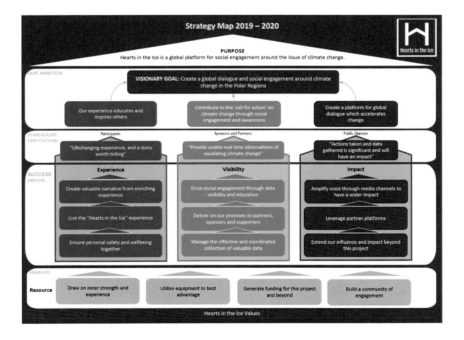

> ## Our experience educates and inspires others

1. We took our collective polar experience and used it to live a remote, simple life for nine months, staying fully present and making every single minute count. We shared our aliveness with all!

2. We lived in harmony with nature, wildlife, and our surroundings. We shared our experiences, our findings, and our love and hopes for our natural world. We hope our experiences and our contribution will inspire others to engage and make a difference.

Contribute to the 'call for action' on climate change through social engagement and awareness

1. We engaged with our partners and sponsors through stories and photos and encouraged everyone to become citizen scientists. We encouraged collaboration across all channels.
2. We communicated with our sponsors, science partners, educators, and followers throughout the world every week, sharing details of our life, magical experiences, research, ideas, and thoughts from our remote trapper's cabin in the Arctic.

Create a platform for global dialogue which accelerates change

1. As a team, we were committed to living with integrity and in alignment with our values, collecting data and fulfilllllling our obligations to science. We were also committed to sharing our remote existence at Bamsebu with others through our blog, social media, and stories in the press.
2. We lived with integrity and a minimal footprint. We built awareness, communication, and a network around the dramatic climate changes in the Arctic. Bamsebu was a hub for our citizen-science contributions, our experiences in nature, our overwintering, and all of our communication about the changes we saw—all of it conveyed with the goal of creating hope and engagement.

And what did we aim to contribute to the climate conversation? Here were some of our goals:

- **Connectivity.** We aimed to remain connected with the world outside of Bamsebu through our website, social media, satellite calls, and networks. We also engaged with our science partners on the data we collected as citizen scientists. We powered our connectivity using solar panels and a windmill and were net-zero for a full year.
- **Education.** We partnered with the amazing Canadian explorer Joe Grabowski of *Exploring by the Seat of Your Pants* to host two calls a month with experts on subjects like weather, the ocean, technology, mental and physical health, wildlife, and more. We reached thousands of youth during the course of our project.
- **Inspiration.** Our rich backgrounds in the polar regions have given us so much experience and knowledge, like a library full of books. We wanted to share our love for life, people, and our planet in everything we do—emails, calls, actions, and, of course, overwintering at Bamsebu.
- **Collaboration.** We wove together people from various backgrounds and specialties who had been working in silos and connected them to leverage data and information.

Who Are You?

That was the "why" of our project, but how about the "who"? We needed to get very clear about our senses of self, our beliefs, and what was important to us to help us focus on our two most precious resources—time and energy.

We asked ourselves the following questions—and we'd encourage you to do the same thing if you're considering embarking on a new project.

What is your purpose?
What do you value?
What do you want?
Where do you want to go?
And what legacy will you leave behind?

Our partners at Strategy Together also helped us create our mission for *Hearts in the Ice* by asking us the following questions:

1. What really fulfilllls you? What was happening in your life at times when you felt fulfilllled? Can you spot any recurring patterns or features?
2. If you had only a year to live, what would you consider to be your most important priorities?
3. What do you want to do with your life that you have not yet done?
4. What is your wish for your children and/or the generations to follow as it relates to climate change?
5. What do you care about, and what will you do about that?

As human beings, we are capable of redirecting our lives by altering the way we think. This involves first taking the time to understand ourselves and then creating change. And while you can't always change the people around you, you can control your reactions to them. As Viktor Frankl said, "Between stimulus and response there is a space. In that space is our power to choose our response. In our response lies our growth and our freedom." Your thoughts are powerful resources, and what you think defines who you are and what you do in every aspect of your life.

Our Call to Action

Our goal has been to take people from climate despair or depression to climate optimism, or a sense of hope and possibility.

It's so hard to stay present in our lives and really live them. Instead, life all too often seems to live us, leaving us old and perhaps sick, looking back with a lot of regrets. With *Hearts in the Ice*, we wanted to wake people up to themselves and this incredible planet we can explore and experience.

The time for waiting and wondering what to do has passed. It's now time to be curious, ask questions, get educated, find a project, issue, or purpose—and then show up. That means vote, volunteer, collect data as a citizen scientist, speak up, and speak out.

We are entering a "perfect storm" of change where individual activists are beginning to shift awareness of the climate crisis and provoke new conversations. These developments must be matched by an evolving model of leadership that's collaborative, inclusive, legacy-minded, and trustworthy.

Change will happen when more leaders lead for the greater good and individual and collective influence (along with external events that will shift what we value) creates greater awareness of the problems we face.

Looking for ways to take action today? Here are some tips from our daily life at Bamsebu:

Connectivity and communication

- Reach out to tell people how much you care about them, what you appreciate about them, and all the things you thank them for. Tell them! Call them. Show you care.
- Write letters or postcards regardless of how long they might take to get to their destination.
- Work things out by talking. If you feel reactive, "let the train pass." Listen. Be clear. Be kind.
- When one of us did something that provoked the other, we would work to set our egos aside and take time to talk or cry it out. We came from a place of love, fondness, and deep mutual respect for each other, and we would try to show that, even when our five-year-old selves showed up.
- "Double-click" when necessary: Ask for clarification to ensure you heard what the other person was trying to communicate.
- Show and express gratitude for small, daily contributions. It might feel unnecessary but acknowledging another person's contribution—whether it's washing up, chopping wood, bringing in ice or snow for water, making dinner or coffee, or taking care of any daily task—makes a huge difference. Even if the person would have made that contribution anyway, being grateful changes the whole atmosphere.
- With limited email and data ability, we read, listened to music, painted, played the ukulele, wrote, played card games, and played football/soccer. It mattered that we took time to play and to share our ideas with each other. This strengthened our friendship and added creative content to our project.
- There's nothing more exciting than learning new things and connecting with people from around the world. Our citizen-science projects enabled us to do that.

- Finding ways to be of service—whether to a neighbor, a project, or a community—gives a sense of purpose and meaning that matters.
- Spending time outside connected to the elements does wonders. Get outside—walk, talk, and play. We were so grateful for the amazing world outside Bamsebu.
- Self-care. It all starts with ourselves: how we feel and think and what we value. Make sure you sleep well.

Problem-solving

- When something broke or stopped working, we would try to be patient and use our creativity to fix it with what we had. There was nobody to call to come and repair a boat engine or a door. Breaking or spilling something wasn't worth getting irritated about—it was just a "thing."
- Change is constant, both at Bamsebu and elsewhere, and adaptability is key. This makes it essential to have good people on your team. We all need each other as we navigate change. When we needed guidance or help, we would reach out to our experts: Carina, Kit, Steinar, Bettina, and our close family and friends.

Creativity

- Reuse. Recycle. Find the hidden treasures packed away in a box, closet, or your storage shed. Shop used clothing or rent them (i.e., fjong.no).
- When your resources are limited, you learn to get creative—to use what you have and share with those who don't. Sunniva lost her favorite knife, and Hilde gave hers up as a gift. All of Hilde's long underwear had holes, so Sunniva gave her a fresh set.
- Shower and wash your clothes less often. Use dry shampoo. Minimize flushing the toilet and consider purchasing a low-flow toilet or a Cinderella incinerator toilet.

With a little planning, you can save money, time, and natural resources, and do your part to avoid climate catastrophe.

When we started this project, we were asked what we wished for on the other end of our stay at Bamsebu. Here's what we said:

> We hope that every single person out there understands that they matter and can make an invaluable contribution. We hope individuals will step up to their own leadership abilities, find a project or "thing" they are passionately curious about, and become citizen scientists.

This experience has been life-changing. It's given us a concrete sense of purpose. We've realized how valuable we can be to others when we lead from the front, not from backstage or the sidelines. Upon reflection, we both feel that we have inspired youth and adults around the world. We took the once in a lifetime opportunity to adventure and experience the Arctic from our little Bamsebu, and we made it count. We've learned how powerful it is when women show up and support each other—and this, in turn, made us want to be better leaders and better people. We've realized how valuable we are as citizen scientists, both to the science community and to the global community, through the stories we shared. We have heard first-hand that many people never knew a thing about citizen science until we introduced them to it. This experience has required us to work together closely and given us the ability to self-reflect as well as seeing ourselves through others' eyes, helping us to continue to evolve in a strategic, thoughtful way.

Time waits for no one. Global warming is happening. We must follow Paul Hawken's lead in thinking of the climate emergency as "an atmospheric transformation" that can inspire us to change, reimagining everything we make and everything we do.

This time of crisis is an opportunity and invitation to build, innovate, collaborate, and use our intellectual flexibility to create change. The climate always has changed and always will. The goal is to come into alignment with the impact we're having on it by investigating the human causes of global warming and ways to reverse it or slow it down.

Climate-change solutions depend on each one of us. *Hearts in the Ice* is just one project that started with two people centered on collaboration, community, inspiration, and cooperation. Through projects like ours, it's proof that individuals can become a movement, and movements can change how we think and see the world, as well as create more evolved social norms. We only have this one home. If we are to stay here, which we are, we must together, as a collective, take great care. We must become a *we* instead of an *I*. A *we* that is unstoppable, kind, courageous, solution-oriented and fearless.

Sunniva searching for wildlife.

Svalbard Reindeer against the sunset in Malbukta.

Proudly displaying our Hearts in the Ice flag during our lunch break.

Two Hearts in the Ice. We protect what we love!

The warm glow from Bamsebu and the brush of northern lights.

Closing the wooden shutters—after a walk in the polar night.

Fall outing Hilde and Ettra—we all loved being outside!

Afternoon snowmobile outing to Rechecherfjorden.

Sunniva in her element—there is no such thing as bad weather!

Hilde's smile says it all—a dream of an overwintering fulfilled!

Hilde and Ettra after a trip to Kapp Fleur de Lys.

What is it like to be Ettra—with 24/7 love from two moms?

Sunniva capturing the iceflow at the shoreline.

The color of the Northern Lights is even more beautiful in person!

Just another day in paradise!

Ever curious Ettra.

RESOURCES

EXPLORING BY THE SEAT OF YOUR PANTS

Together with *Exploring by the Seat of Your Pants, Hearts in the Ice* connected with thousands of youth from around the world on topics such as technology, weather, biodiversity, polar bears, climate change, mental and physical health, and the power of community. For each call, we consulted an expert with global reach. All calls were recorded and can be found at www.exploringbytheseat.com/hiti/ and www.heartsintheice. com/education/.

Citizen-science projects

You can follow the citizen-science projects we contributed to at:

- *Hearts in the Ice* Citizen Science: www.heartsintheice.com/ citizen-science/
- NASA's Aurorasaurus: www.aurorasaurus.org
- NASA's GLOBE Observer: https://observer.globe.gov
- Scripps Institution of Oceanography's Fjord Phyto: https://fjord-phyto.ucsd.edu

For general information on citizen science and projects to join:

- Citizen Science Association: www.citizenscience.org
- SciStarter, Lists more than 3,000 citizen-science projects: www. scistarter.org
- BioBlitz events, Concentrated surveys of native plants and animals in a particular area by scientists, citizen scientists, and the general public: www.nationalgeographic.org/projects/bioblitz/
- iNaturalist, A social network connecting researchers and nature enthusiasts, app available for download: www.iNaturalist.org
- Litterati, A global garbage-clean-up community, app available for download: www.litterati.org
- Aurora Forecast 3D, App available for download to track aurora sightings around the world: http://kho.unis.no/Forecast3D.htm
- BackyardBio, A citizen-science documenting project run on iNaturalist by Exploring by the Seat of Your Pants: www.inaturalist.org/ projects/backyardbio
- eBird, Tracks bird sightings, app available for download: www. ebird.org

BIBLIOGRAPHY

Anette and Susanne Bastviken, *Jordnært*

Rachel Carson, *Silent Spring*

Darlene Cavalier and Eric B. Kennedy, *The Rightful Place of Science: Citizen Science*

Mihaly Csikszentmihalyi, *Finding Flow: The Psychology of Engagement with Everyday Life*

Viktor Frankl, *Man's Search for Meaning*

Paul Hawken, *Drawdown: The Most Comprehensive Plan Ever Proposed to Reverse Global Warming*

Barry Lopez, *Arctic Dreams*

Christiane Ritter, *A Woman in the Polar Night*

David Rock, *Your Brain at Work*

Jason Scotts, *Mental Focus and Brain Games for Memory Improvement*

Rolf Stange, *Rocks and Ice: Landscapes of the North*

Rolf Stange, *Spitsbergen–Svalbard: A Complete Guide Around the Arctic Archipelago*

Melanie Windridge, *Aurora: In Search of the Northern Lights*

Our science and education partners, and other organizations to support

- Norwegian Polar Institute: www.npolar.no

- Polar Bears International: www.PolarBearsInternational.org
- The Jane Goodall Institute: www.JaneGoodall.org
- David Suzuki Foundation: www.DavidSuzuki.org
- CHOOSE, Carbon offsets and other climate solutions for businesses: www.chooose.today
- Canopy, Protecting our forests: www.canopyplanet.org
- EAT, Science-based global platform for food system transformation: www.EATForum.org
- Roots & Shoots, Empowering young people to affect positive change in their communities (founded by Jane Goodall): www.RootsandShoots.org
- Tomorrow's Air, Collective for carbon removal service for global travelers: www.tomorrowsair.com
- American Geophysical Union: www.agu.org

Leadership/inspiration

- Kit Jackson at Strategy Together: www.strategytogether.com
- Carina Vinberg at Framgångare: www.framgangare.se
- Fabian Dattner at Homeward Bound: www.homewardboundprojects.com.au
- WINGS WorldQuest: www.wingsworldquest.org
- Society of Woman Geographers: www.iswg.org
- The Explorers Club: www.explorers.org
- Global Choices: www.globalchoices.org
- Nacho Dean: www.nachodean.com
- TED Countdown: https://countdown.ted.com/